CHILD SEXUAL ABUSE

Other Books in the At Issue Series:

CHILD SEXUAL ABUSE

David Bender, *Publisher*
Bruno Leone, *Executive Editor*

Brenda Stalcup, *Managing Editor*
Scott Barbour, *Series Editor*

Paul A. Winters, *Book Editor*

An Opposing Viewpoints® Series

Greenhaven Press, Inc.
San Diego, California

Library of Congress Cataloging-in-Publication Data

Child sexual abuse / Paul A. Winters, book editor.
  p.   cm. — (At issue)
  Includes bibliographical references and index.
  ISBN 1-56510-689-X (lib. : alk. paper). —
ISBN 1-56510-688-1 (pbk. : alk. paper)
  1. Child sexual abuse—United States. 2. Sexually abused
children—United States. 3. Child molesters—United States.
I. Winters, Paul A., 1965– . II. Series: At issue
(San Diego, Calif.)
HV6570.2.C55   1998
362.76'0973—dc21   97-27516
                                                             CIP

© 1998 by Greenhaven Press, Inc., PO Box 289009,
San Diego, CA 92198-9009

Printed in the U.S.A.

Table of Contents

Introduction

The problem of child sexual abuse has attracted a great deal of attention in recent years. The American media have reported numerous cases in which persons in positions of trust—including day care providers, clergymen, and scout leaders—have been accused (and in some cases convicted) of molesting children under their care. Many of these charges have been made by adults who claim to have recovered repressed memories of abuse they were subjected to as children. Other widely reported stories have involved children being abused—and sometimes murdered—by convicted child molesters newly released from prison. In addition, pedophiles have reportedly lured child victims into abusive situations via the Internet. Commentators point to such developments as evidence that the problem of child sexual abuse in the United States is alarmingly serious.

On the other hand, some researchers and social critics, while agreeing that child sexual abuse is a horrendous crime, maintain that the extent of the problem has been exaggerated due to various causes. Media critics contend that intensive reporting of a few sensational cases has created a sense of panic among the public. Others question the validity of the recovered memories that are the basis of many child abuse accusations. In addition, the victimization of children, society's most vulnerable members, automatically provokes intense anger among parents and concerned citizens who demand action on the part of law enforcement. While such outrage is natural and understandable, some commentators argue that the public's response to recent developments has been excessive and has created the impression that the problem is worse than it actually is.

Varying estimates

This debate remains unresolved in part because it is impossible to determine the exact extent of the problem. Experts believe that most cases of child sexual abuse are never reported to authorities. In fact, the FBI has estimated that only 1 percent to 10 percent of child sexual abuse cases are reported to the police. Children often do not report being sexually abused because they are ashamed, are afraid of repercussions, or are reluctant to betray their abusers. In addition, many reports of child sexual abuse are never substantiated, either because they are unfounded or because they cannot be proven. Child sexual abuse cases are frequently difficult to prove due to a lack of physical evidence (especially if the abuse is reported a significant period of time after it occurred) or due to unreliable testimony by the child victim. For these reasons, estimates of the prevalence of child sexual abuse vary wildly. Ann Wolbert Burgess and Christine A. Grant of the University of Pennsylvania School of Nursing report that in nine scientific studies they reviewed, the prevalence of sexual abuse ranged from 6 percent to 62 percent for girls and from 3 percent to 31 percent for boys.

Some researchers contend that the high estimates of child sexual abuse reported by a number of studies are exaggerated, due in part to overreporting by professionals who work with children. Current law requires those who supervise or treat children, such as teachers and doctors, to report any and all possible cases of child abuse to law enforcement authorities. These professionals are immune from prosecution if they make mistaken allegations but are liable for criminal penalties if they fail to report a case. This "mandated reporting," according to Richard A. Gardner, a clinical professor of child psychiatry at Columbia University, has resulted in "overreporting of even the most absurd and impossible allegations." Gardner and other critics of mandated reporting laws maintain that this overreporting by professionals has led to inflated statistics on child sexual abuse.

Critics contend that the problem of overreporting is compounded by the manner in which reports are handled by child protection agencies and investigators. Social workers are frequently accused of being too eager to believe charges of abuse, to remove children from their homes, and to subject parents to intensive scrutiny. In addition, child protection officials have received a great deal of criticism for their performance in a number of highly publicized child sexual abuse cases, such as the McMartin Preschool case in Manhattan Beach, California, in which two defendants were tried and subsequently acquitted on charges of molesting dozens of children. According to K.L. Billingsly, a fellow at the Center for Popular Culture, videotaped interviews with the children in that case revealed that therapists used "coercive methods" and "manipulated the children into making false accusations." Critics point to this and similar cases to substantiate their assertion that child protective service agencies are overly zealous in their investigation and prosecution of child sexual abuse accusations, thereby exaggerating the scope of the problem.

Underreported and lightly prosecuted

Many others counter that child sexual abuse is an underreported problem. As noted previously, most experts agree that the majority of cases of abuse are never reported by the victim. Moreover, the National Center for Prosecution of Child Abuse disputes the contention that professionals overreport abuse. The center maintains that many of those who are mandated to report suspected abuse "do not report serious cases because they do not believe the child protection or legal systems will follow up the case effectively." In short, according to the center, professionals are underreporting rather than overreporting the problem of child sexual abuse.

Moreover, many commentators defend child protective service agencies against claims that they are too eager to believe reports of child sexual abuse. According to the National Center for Prosecution of Child Abuse, "Up to 60% of child sexual abuse reports are not even believed." The center also rejects the argument that child sexual abuse cases are investigated and prosecuted with excessive zeal. Due to the difficulty in proving such charges, according to the center, "suspects arrested for sexual offenses against children are less likely to be prosecuted than other violent offenders." In one study of sexual abuse allegations in day care centers, 82 percent of the charges were dismissed, the center reports. The center also notes that those convicted of child sexual abuse are given relatively light sentences; only 19 percent receive sentences of more than one year.

Disagreement regarding the reporting and prosecution of child sexual abuse cases reflects deeper dissension about the extent of the problem in American society. The contributors to *At Issue: Child Sexual Abuse* examine the prevalence of child sexual abuse, the reliability of recovered memories of abuse, the seriousness of the problem of child abuse committed by other children, and whether priests who have molested children can be reintegrated into society. By focusing on these issues, the authors in this anthology confront one of the most disturbing and destructive crimes that society faces—the sexual violation of children.

1

The Prevalence of Child Sexual Abuse: An Overview

Cheryl Wetzstein

Cheryl Wetzstein is a journalist for the Washington Times.

Many U.S. citizens favor locking up child molesters and keeping them in jail forever. However, attempting to identify dangerous pedophiles presents a dilemma. Child molesters suffer a diversity of sexual disorders that are difficult to clinically diagnose, making it nearly impossible for psychiatrists to determine which abusers will commit repeat offenses. Since the mid-1980s efforts have been made to collect statistics on the extent of child abuse, but the data suffer from both exaggeration and underreporting.

"I got away with molesting over 240 children before getting caught for molesting just one little boy," convicted child molester Larry Don McQuay has confessed.

"With all that I have coldheartedly learned while in prison, there is no way that I will ever be caught again," he has said. "I am doomed to eventually rape, then murder my poor little victims to keep them from telling on me. . . . Will your children be my next victims?"

These words led to headlines in April 1996 when McQuay was ordered released from a Texas jail after serving six years of an eight-year prison sentence for the 1989 rape of a six-year-old boy. He had served his time, according to Texas' mandatory-release rules.

Before McQuay was taken to a halfway house to prepare for his reentry into society, he pleaded to be castrated to lessen his sexual drive. A victims' rights group in Houston, called Justice for All, began a fundraising campaign to meet McQuay's request but could not find a doctor who would perform the unusual surgery to remove the testicles. McQuay has since been returned to jail on charges stemming from a previous molestation case.

The case of Larry Don McQuay seems to epitomize society's continuing inability to deal with those who have incorrigible and unspeakable appetites for children.

From Cheryl Wetzstein, "The Child Molestation Dilemma." This article appeared in the December 1996 issue and is reprinted with permission from the *World & I*, a publication of The Washington Times Corporation, copyright ©1996.

9

One obvious permanent solution—capital punishment—is strictly reserved for murder and is likely to remain so. The public remains divided over the merits of the death penalty, child sexual abuse cases are difficult to prove beyond all question of doubt, and most sex offenders are members of or known to the victim's family, making the latter unlikely to call for a death sentence.

As a result, there is a push to sentence child molesters to life in prison without parole or place them in secure mental institutions until they are judged not to be a danger to society.

In the meantime, however, many offenders receive probation or short prison sentences, and thousands are released from jail and back into society each year.

Recidivism rates

The chances a sex offender will commit another crime seem to depend on the nature of his sexual appetite.

In January 1996, *Congressional Quarterly* reported that, according to international research findings, including a 1994 paper issued by the Washington State Institute for Public Policy, recidivism rates for untreated sex offenders ranged as follows:

- 41 to 71 percent for exhibitionists;
- 13 to 40 percent for child molesters preferring boy victims;
- 10 to 29 percent for child molesters preferring girl victims;
- 7 to 35 percent for rapists;
- 4 to 10 percent for incest offenders.

Some medical experts hold that sex offenders can be successfully treated.

"I don't think the majority [of sex offenders] have a condition that's curable, but I do think that many of them have a psychiatric disorder and can, like alcoholics, learn to control themselves and live safely in the community," Fred Berlin, director of the National Institute for the Study, Prevention and Treatment of Sexual Trauma in Baltimore, Maryland, told *Congressional Quarterly*.

But others are not at all sure that pedophiles—people whose sexual preference is for children—can ever live "safely" in society.

"Pedophiles are always model prisoners and want parole," said John Walsh, whose young son was abducted and found murdered many years ago. The show he hosted for years—Fox-TV's *America's Most Wanted*—once helped catch 37 pedophiles accused of crimes in one six-month period, he said. Ninety percent of them were repeat offenders.

The most worrisome sort of offender is the pedophile who molests, known to law enforcement officials as a "preferential child molester."

"When you find out how they've conducted their lives, you realize it's their whole life to molest," said Patrick Trueman, former chief of the Department of Justice's Child Exploitation and Obscenity Section and now director of governmental affairs for the American Family Association.

Trueman and others, noting that even notorious offenders seem to get only eight-year prison sentences, strongly believe in very long prison terms, if not life in prison.

Diversity of disorders

The diversity of sexual disorders has made both clinical diagnosis and uniform legal responses difficult.

For example, virtually all pedophiles collect child pornography, fantasize about children, and engage in infantile or abnormal behavior around them. But not all pedophiles actually assault children. They may instead employ means of self-gratification that are not illegal.

Adults who assault children are child molesters, but not all child molesters are pedophiles. Some child molesters are sexual predators who prefer adult victims but attack a child because an opportunity appears. Such "situational child molesters" are believed to be the most common kind of offender but the least likely to abuse large numbers of children.

Instead, the most worrisome sort of offender is the pedophile who molests, known to law enforcement officials as a "preferential child molester." Such a man is likely to be involved in child pornography, sex rings, and child prostitution. He may molest hundreds or even a thousand children in a lifetime, wrote FBI Supervisory Special Agent Kenneth Lanning in a 1992 booklet issued by the National Center for Missing and Exploited Children (NCMEC).

It is frankly impossible to determine how extensive child sexual abuse is.

Referring to a landmark, long-term study of 561 sex offenders by Dr. Gene Abel, an Atlanta sexual disorder expert, Lanning said that pedophiles who targeted boys outside the home committed the greatest number of crimes, with an average of 281.7 acts with an average of 150.2 partners.

Molesters who targeted girls within the family committed an average of 81.3 acts with an average of 1.8 partners. The Abel study also found that nearly a quarter of the 561 subjects committed crimes against both family and nonfamily members, Lanning wrote in *Child Molesters: A Behavioral Analysis*.

A number of punishments have been suggested for child sex offenders, but all have drawbacks.

Meanwhile, nearly every state has enacted laws requiring sex offenders to register in their new homes. Such laws have faced court challenges by civil liberties advocates who argue that sex offenders who have paid their debt to society deserve to rejoin it without undue constraints.

Registration laws have withstood many of these challenges, however, and in May 1996 President Clinton signed the so-called Megan's Law, which requires states to tell local law enforcement officials and communities when a convicted sex offender has moved in.

The law was named for Megan Kanka, a New Jersey seven-year-old who in 1994 was raped and murdered by a twice-convicted sex offender who lived across the street and whose background was unknown to the Kankas or their neighbors.

The quest for data

"Society's attitude about child sexual abuse and exploitation can be summed up in one word: denial," Lanning wrote in a 1992 analysis on child sex rings.

"Most people do not want to hear about it and would prefer to pretend that child sexual victimization just does not occur," he wrote, urging professionals who deal with child sexual abuse to recognize and deal with this denial.

But the flip side of denial is public hysteria—and professionals must also be aware that there can be a lot of misinformation about the subject, Lanning said in his report.

"Some professionals . . . in their zeal to make American society more aware of this victimization, tend to exaggerate the problem," Lanning wrote. "Presentations and literature with poorly documented or misleading claims about one in three children being sexually molested, the $5 billion child pornography industry, child slavery rings, and 50,000 stranger-abducted children are not uncommon.

"The problem is bad enough; it is not necessary to exaggerate it," Lanning concluded.

Efforts have been under way to collect reliable data on missing and exploited children since 1984, when Congress passed the Juvenile Justice, Runaway Youth, and Missing Children's Act Amendments, creating NCMEC in Arlington, Virginia, and instituting the National Incidence Studies of Missing, Abducted, Runaway and Thrownaway Children (NISMART).

NISMART estimates that, each year:

- 450,000 children, most of whom are teenagers, run away from home and stay away at least one night.
- 354,000 children are abducted by a family member, typically a noncustodial parent.
- 127,100 children are "thrown away," that is, abandoned or ejected from their homes.
- 114,600 cases of attempted abduction by a nonfamily member are reported.
- 3,200 to 4,600 children are reported abducted by nonfamily members.

Nonfamily abductors include persons who are known to the child (that is, a neighbor or family friend), or unknown, namely, strangers. But the most common scenario, according to NISMART data, involves someone using a weapon to force a child from the street into a vehicle.

Most of these nonfamily abductions last less than 24 hours, but two-thirds of cases involve a sexual assault. Half of the abducted children are teenagers, and 75 percent are girls. The highest percentage of victims appears to be girls aged 11–14 and boys aged 6–9.

Each year, between 200 and 300 children taken by strangers are gone for long periods. About half of the children are recovered alive, usually within two months. But each year, between 43 and 147 children abducted by nonfamily members are found dead, according to NISMART's review of data from 1976 to 1987.

Familiar offenders

It's not only strangers who molest children, however. Sexual abusers include parents, grandparents, siblings, other family members, stepparents, family friends, and other responsible adults in close contact with children such as teachers, Scout leaders, clergymen, and coaches.

With abuse coming from so many directions, it's easy to assume that child sexual abuse is epidemic. Certainly, the endless parade of abuse survivors on daytime talk shows provides anecdotal evidence that the problem is "everywhere." And when the amount of unreported abuse is added in—an FBI document says that "only 1 to 10 percent of child molestation cases are ever reported to police"—it indeed appears that there must be a child molester on every block.

But it is frankly impossible to determine how extensive child sexual abuse is. The National Committee for the Prevention of Child Abuse said a few years ago: "Retrospective surveys reveal great variation [in the national rate of abuse], with 6 percent to 62 percent of females and 3 percent to 31 percent of males reporting to have experienced some form of sexual abuse."

The burden of proof

Finally, it would be easier to toughen the laws against child molesting if more people were diagnosed as incorrigible child molesters. But those who try to prosecute child sexual abuse cases run into a vast array of hurdles.

In most instances of sexual abuse—three out of four documented cases, according to one reputable study published in 1994—there are no physical marks or signs of abuse.

This places the burden of proof on other signs of distress—for example, bed-wetting, sexual precociousness, and withdrawal. But these can be attributed to other causes.

Then there is the victim's testimony. But testimony from children is notoriously unreliable. They may be too young to talk or confused about what happened to them. They may be reluctant to betray the "special secret" they share with their abuser or may blame themselves, having been told "you wanted it" by the abuser. They also may be unduly influenced by their parents, therapists, law enforcement officials, or others and make allegations that are eventually recanted or discounted.

While most victims of abuse do not forget their molestation, some may repress such memories and not recall it until years later, either through some spontaneous event or through therapy.

Cases of such "recovered memories" have made sensational stories in recent years. Adult children have recalled being abused by their parents, and men have remembered being abused by their clergymen. Some of these cases have led to arrests, convictions, or multimillion-dollar lawsuits for damages. At least 21 states have extended the statute of limitations for sexual abuse so those who belatedly wish to take legal action against their abuser can do so.

But some cases have sparked a fierce outcry from those accused. In March 1992, a group called the False Memory Syndrome Foundation, located in Philadelphia, arose to help rebut what it said were distorted or confabulated memories contrived through incompetent therapy.

As a result of this and other controversies, convictions in sexual abuse cases are not only difficult to get but may be difficult to uphold.

"The reality," says David Beatty, a spokesman with the National Victim Center in Arlington, Virginia, "is that people victimize children because they feel like they can get away with it."

If society becomes better educated about sexual abuse of children, he said, it will at least increase the likelihood that predators will be caught and punished.

Child Sexual Abuse Is
a Widespread Problem

Andrew Vachss

Andrew Vachss is a children's attorney in New York City.

The revelation over recent decades that child sexual abuse is a widespread phenomenon has prompted a backlash led by people who maintain that they have been wrongly accused of this heinous crime. Despite the possibility of false accusations and inconvenience to families, however, a thorough investigation should be conducted whenever an allegation of child molestation is made. Further, more resources should be devoted to protecting children from sexual abuse.

S ome people will tell you that there was no such thing as child sexual abuse a few short decades ago—the "good old days." And if you go to the files and read the old newspapers, you might well believe them.

Unless you were a victim, now grown to adulthood.

Media coverage of child abuse

Then the media "discovered" child abuse. Like a pendulum, press coverage swung from one extreme to the other. From being reported so rarely that many doubted its very existence, child abuse became such a frequent subject of coverage that rarely a day went by without new accounts of horrors.

Now the media spotlight has been turned on defendants who maintain that they have been falsely accused of sexually abusing children—and the media backlash is so strong that you might well believe that we are in the midst of a modern-day Salem witch hunt.

Here's the truth: The battle against child sexual abuse is no "witch hunt." In Salem, there *were* no witches. In 20th-century America, sexual predators *do* exist—in alarming numbers.

Blaming the media won't make the problem go away. The media didn't invent child sexual abuse, and it can't make it disappear. Nor will our collective wishing make it do so. In fact, taking the ostrich approach actually benefits predators. Ignorance helps them to multiply, and cowardice makes them strong.

There are far more people who love and respect children than there are those who prey upon them. But if that is so, why aren't we winning this battle? Because, with all the media muddle surrounding child abuse, we are losing confidence in our collective ability to find out the truth.

How do we learn that truth? How do we protect our children?

A child abuse case is never a level playing field. It is never a fair fight. Why? What is so special about children that we treat these cases differently from other vicious crimes? Is it true that children's "memories" are different from those of adults? That children are easily "brainwashed" or cannot distinguish between truth and fantasy? Or is it that children are perceived as property, as lesser citizens, because of their age? Do we fear the inadequacy of their memories—or the truth of them?

If we want the truth about child sexual abuse, there is just one thing we can do: Look only *at the facts of each individual case.*

I have never yet met an abused child (of whatever age) who was not crying to be heard and to be believed, to be validated and (eventually) assured that there was nothing "special" about him or her that brought on the abuse—that the child was simply a "parent's" (or other predator's) target of opportunity.

Child abuse cases *are* different, in part because the stakes are so much higher. If an adult is the victim of a crime, even if the defendant is acquitted, the adult is as "free" as the perpetrator. But in a child abuse case, the consequences of an improper acquittal are often that the victim is returned to the abuser.

The major difference between child abuse cases and all others is this: Those who make the decisions—be they judges, juries, social workers, police officers or the general public—too often act as though the "issue" were on trial, not the facts. But child sexual abuse is not an "issue," like capital punishment or abortion or gun control. Child abuse is a fact—a hideous, foul fact that traumatizes our culture just as it traumatizes individual victims.

If we want the truth about child sexual abuse, there is just one thing we can do: Look *only* at the facts of each individual case. It is not a question of "believing" children, or of "believing" in "witch hunts" or "false allegations." It is, and always will be, a question of fact-finding.

It sounds cold-blooded to say this, but a wrongful conviction of child abuse can be reversed. The damage from a wrongful acquittal probably cannot. Unless and until we learn to judge, case-by-case—unless and until we work to create a climate in which the facts *will* be found—countless victims will continue to be doomed.

Protecting one's own children is a biological imperative—it is how our species sustains itself. When an animal fails to protect its babies, they do not survive. And so the negative characteristics of that unprotective parent are not carried forth into new generations.

But it doesn't work that way with human beings. Our minds have evolved ways to sustain ourselves even when we ignore our biological imperatives. Children can no longer rely on our "instincts" for protection. Only our *actions* can achieve that goal.

For every parent who violates the sacred trust *every* child represents, there are thousands committed not only to protecting their children but also to protecting *all* children. That desire is our highest calling. The actual expression of that desire defines the character of each individual. And we can only truly express such a desire with behavior—rhetoric won't get the job done.

Healthy, happy, productive children—children who evoke their maximum potential—are no accident. They are not some fortuitous result of randomly scattering seeds on unnourishing ground. No, such children are always a harvested blessing, deeply dependent on climate and care. We create that climate and that care; and its most precious, indispensable element is *safety*.

Calling children "our most precious resource" is easy. Treating them as such is the key to our species.

More cases of child sexual abuse are *never* reported than are *ever* tried. Yes, some people are wrongfully convicted. And we must do our best to see that this never happens and to rectify it when it does. But no child benefits from being forced to carry the banner of a false allegation. Being made to do so is, in itself, a pernicious form of child abuse. And, every day, innocent victims are being ignored even when their cases do come to court.

What happens to those children?

Your children, America.

The need for resources to fight child abuse

We need to pay what it costs to find the truth, because we can't afford what it costs not to. The best—indeed, the *only*—way to protect our children is to increase radically the resources available.

We need therapy for all children who are the subject of child abuse allegations, regardless of any jury voting "guilty" or "not guilty."

We need better investigations. That means better investigators. And that means comprehensive training. It means adequate pay, competent supervision and full accountability. It means the use of standardized protocols, so that the outcome depends on the facts, not on the individual perspective of the investigator.

We need an objective "one-stop shop" system to avoid the confusion that results from subjecting a child to a series of interviews. All cases would be referred to a multidisciplinary resource center which has no vested interest in the outcome and which has the sole job of finding the facts. No party to the case—be it prosecution, defense, a parent in a custody battle or otherwise—would be permitted to control the investigation. A full and complete record should be made available to all once it is finished.

For children especially, investigative interviewing to determine the likelihood of sexual abuse is an inherently intrusive and often traumatic experience. Because they want the pain to stop, many children go "mute" or "stop remembering," making it appear that they are changing their account of the events. And any such disparities can easily be exploited.

We need a system in which only wrongdoers fear the consequences.

It took an informed and enraged nation to pass child labor laws. It will take no less to protect children from an even more horrific societal crime.

We humans have been on the planet a long time. If we forget where we come from, if we forget our own children, then our evolution is not "in progress"—it is finished.

3

Child Sexual Abuse Is Not Widespread

K.L. Billingsley

K.L. Billingsley is a fellow at the Center for the Study of Popular Culture in Los Angeles.

Concern over child abuse has produced a form of hysteria, and false accusations and unfair prosecutions have become common. In some cases, such as the McMartin preschool case in Los Angeles, the work of manipulative therapists has encouraged young children to invent outrageous tales of satanic abuse. In less high-profile cases, child protective service personnel and civil prosecutors have violated the due process rights of accused parents and have torn families apart on the basis of unsupported suspicions and flimsy evidence.

Child abuse, especially of a sexual nature, has been a high-profile issue in recent years and has now acquired celebrity status. In his internationally publicized row with Mia Farrow, Woody Allen found himself staring down the barrel of child-abuse accusations. In May 1991, former Miss America Marilyn Van Derbur Atler accused her late father of sexually abusing her as a child. Roseanne Arnold made similar claims, soon to be repeated by Angle Dickinson, Cindy Williams, Desi Arnaz, Jr., and others. "Soon, remembered childhood abuse had become an explanation for whatever ailed an unhappy or maladjusted individual," says Richard Brzustowicz, Jr., coordinator of the Behavioral Research Ethics Review at the University of Washington, adding that before long everyone in Hollywood was "in recovery" from childhood sexual abuse.

The mantra of the sexual-abuse recovery movement, says Brzustowicz, is: "If you think you were abused, you were." On the other hand, the national "war on child abuse," waged by a vast network of organizations and agencies, flies under a different banner that may be summarized as: "If you think someone is a child abuser, he is."

No one denies that child abuse is a serious problem, and only a misanthropic anarchist would deny the state a role in the protection of innocent lives. That task is a difficult one. Consider the case of three-year-old Christa Hawkins, who was hospitalized in 1987 with a fractured ankle, broken arm, and massive bruises. Medical examiners believed the injuries were not accidental and contacted social service agencies. The child went into foster care but was subsequently returned to her mother and abusive stepfather, a Navy man, over the child's objections. Before long, Christa was back at the hospital. Her stepfather had beaten her to death. Though the man was found guilty of murder by torture and sentenced to twenty-five years, one can imagine the guilt of those who had released the child into harm's way and their determination not to let it happen again.

The child-abuse myth

But is child abuse, as one agency claims, an "American tradition" and currently at epidemic levels? After all, according to figures that are often quoted, one in five boys and one in three girls are abused by their parents. But the research arm of the National Committee to Prevent Child Abuse says that these figures have not been substantiated and amount to "a rumor." And Richard Wexler, author of *Wounded Innocents: The Real Victims of the War Against Child Abuse,* points out that between 95 and 99 out of every 100 women were not sexually abused by fathers or stepfathers during childhood. More than 99 out of 100 children, he says, are not beaten up by their parents. And more than 97 percent of all children are not abused or neglected in any way. These figures, says Wexler, come from the same studies the child savers use but fail to cite.

At the same time, the twin creeds of the child-abuse war are combining to wreak havoc of their own, both on innocent individuals and civil liberties. According to Richard Gardner, clinical professor of child psychiatry at Columbia University and an expert on the sexual abuse of children, the United States appears to be witnessing "its third great wave of hysteria." The professor notes the damage of the Salem witch trials and McCarthy hearings but believes that our current child-abuse hysteria "is by far the worst with regard to the number of lives that have been destroyed and families that have disintegrated."

We live in an era, says Dorothy Rabinowitz of the *Wall Street Journal,* "that has elevated certain accusations to the status of the sacrosanct," primarily "racial bias and sex abuse." These charges, says Rabinowitz, "are considered sufficient unto themselves, and beyond, simply because they have been brought." It takes just one accusation to bring forth "cadres of abuse specialists" who find even more charges.

As a result, child-abuse accusations are becoming a national pastime, particularly in divorce and custody cases. By the careful count of Wexler, the number of false child-abuse accusations exceeds one million per year. In view of the short public attention span, some case review is in order.

In August 1983, a Manhattan Beach, California, woman named Judy Johnson told the police that one Raymond Buckey had sexually molested her son. The police sent a form letter to over two hundred families informing them of an investigation of the Buckey family, which ran the McMartin preschool. The letter prejudiced the parents' minds before any formal charges had been filed, and soon wild tales of sexual and satanic abuse were swirling around Los Angeles and the nation, shamelessly played up by the media. So eager to take action was District Attorney Robert Philibosian that he pressed charges while the investigation was yet in progress.

The number of false child-abuse accusations exceeds one million per year.

The sensational nature of the charges diverted attention from the reliability of the accuser. While the case dragged on, Johnson accused five other men, including her husband, of molesting her son. She also charged that an official of the Los Angeles school board had been involved in the crimes. And a U.S. Marine, she said, had broken into her home and sodomized the family dog! Unfortunately, the accuser did not get her day in court. A heavy drinker, Johnson died of a liver ailment before the trial began, and her son did not testify. Judge William Pounders refused to allow subsequent testimony about Johnson's "problems."

To make their case, the authorities relied on 360 interviews of the McMartin children by then-unlicensed therapist Kee MacFarlane and her associates at the Children's Institute International. CII personnel used puppets, leading questions, and other subtly coercive methods to get the children to tell their "yucky stories." Brzustowicz compares the methods with a "16th century manual for ferreting out Satan's consorts." The techniques, he says, "confuse and frighten children" and offer rewards for accusations, sometimes even candy or toys.

Videotapes of the interviews convinced the McMartin jury that the CII therapists had manipulated the children into making false accusations, the same thing that happened in a celebrated Minnesota case under zealous prosecutor Kathleen Morris, who declared herself "sick to death of things like the presumption of innocence," a strange view for someone sworn to uphold the Constitution. In the McMartin case, three children refused to testify and the prosecution dismissed thirty-five charges.

In January 1990, after the longest trial in American history, more than $15 million in court costs, thousands of pages of testimony, and widespread hysteria, a jury acquitted Peggy McMartin Buckey and her son Raymond on forty counts of child molestation. District Attorney Ira Reiner described the legal marathon as "insane," adding: "We have a justice system that, quite frankly, does not work."

Sickness in the child-protection system

Not all such cases receive similar publicity in a system where, to protect juveniles, confidentiality rules and gag orders are standard practice. One exception is San Diego, where a grand jury has been looking into abuses by the child-protection system since the late 1980s. The jury conducted extensive research based on hundreds of interviews with people in all facets of the system. The resulting reports merit serious attention and coincide remarkably with national studies such as *Wounded Innocents*. For example, the San Diego jurors found that approximately 60 percent of the child-abuse cases did not even need to be in the system, roughly the same percentage of false accusations that Wexler discovered on a national scale.

Child-protection authorities knew that Albert Raymond Carder, a convicted child molester, had been entering bedroom windows and raping girls. Yet when a girl in the same neighborhood, Alicia Wade, told a similar story in 1989, they ignored her testimony and charged that her father, Navy man James Wade, had raped his own daughter. They based their suspicions on what they wrongly perceived as a delay in reporting the crime and certain "red flags" they believed pointed to family abuse. These included the fact that it was a military family, that the parents were both overweight, that Wade once had a drinking problem, and that his wife, Denise, had herself been abused as a child.

At the same time, they ignored all the positive aspects of the family. They did not mention that the father's drinking was not a source of problems and that he had not been drinking the day of the attack. There was no reference to Wade's Navy record, which, except for his weight problem, was described as "superb" and "excellent." Reports ignored the mother's day-care business, which ran with no problems, and there were no interviews of these children's parents. Reports failed to mention that Alicia was an A student who had just been named Student of the Month. No one at Alicia's school was interviewed. There was no mention of family participation in community and church activities.

Children's Institute International . . . personnel used puppets, leading questions, and other subtly coercive methods to get the children to tell their "yucky stories."

As for Alicia, she repeatedly denied that her father had been involved and provided a detailed description of her attacker that pointed to Carder. A footprint left outside Alicia's window also matched Carder's shoe size. These facts had little effect on those in the system, who, perhaps remembering victims such as Christa Hawkins, prefer to grab the children first and ask questions later. In the trade, removal of a child is known as a "parentectomy."

Social workers seized Alicia and farmed her out to therapist Kathleen Goodfriend of the La Mesa Village Counseling Group. As a grand jury report noted, Goodfriend's efforts focused on one object: getting the child to name an "acceptable perpetrator," namely the father. This, said the grand jury, was "the only response the system was apparently looking for," although the jurors were also disturbed that Goodfriend taught Alicia about masturbation "without any parental input or apparent interest by the child." Until Alicia accused her father, she, like her parents, was "in denial," an incantation used to make the presumption of innocence disappear. The child-abuse system often presumes guilt and, in effect, forces the accused to prove their innocence.

Goodfriend also got one of Alicia's foster mothers to pressure Alicia, kind of a tag-team effect. Alicia later testified that, after thirteen months of this treatment, coupled with isolation from her family, she finally caved in just to get the therapist off her back. This "disclosure," made under duress, brought all the "therapy" to a screeching halt. The foster parents immediately whisked Alicia off to Disneyland, an obvious reward for delivering the requisite lines. Faced with a hostage situation, the Wades submitted to various tests to prove their innocence and get their child back.

Virtually all men accused of child abuse in San Diego must endure a stretch on the penile plethysmograph, a device now used in a number of states and on boys as young as ten in Arizona. A therapist wires the accused to a machine and subjects him to a procession of erotica that may include child pornography. The test supposedly indicates a "pattern of arousal." During the 1960s the communist government of Czechoslovakia used the device to weed out those using claims of homosexuality to dodge military service. A version is now being developed for women. Since they handle other people's children, often without supervision, it would seem sensible to use the plethysmograph on workers in the system, a measure not currently practiced.

Meanwhile, the child protectors were planning to terminate the Wades' parental rights and have Alicia adopted. They also threatened to seize their son Joshua. Then long-neglected evidence came to light in the form of Alicia's semen-stained panties. DNA tests on these proved that Wade could not have been the attacker. Carder, on the other hand, was among the 5 percent of the population who fit the DNA profile.

Ironically, Deputy County Counsel E. Jane Via, who knew about Carder when she worked for the DA's office, continued to ignore Carder and go after Wade. Even after Wade had been exonerated, Via pushed to have Alicia adopted based on an earlier plea-bargain charge of neglect. It was only the intervention of the grand jury that saved Alicia from being adopted away forever. After two and a half years, the system that purportedly was operating in Alicia's best interest returned the child home. At this time she was using a medicine to which she was allergic, was without the glasses she wore when taken from her parents, and had no record of an ophthalmologist's checkup.

> *Those in the [child-protection] system, . . . perhaps remembering victims such as Christa Hawkins, prefer to grab the children first and ask questions later.*

Wade had become an outcast in the community, and the legal fees robbed him of his life savings and those of his parents. The couple had been deprived of their daughter during a crucial formative period in her life. In spite of the court's "true finding of innocence" for Wade, only one person in the system apologized, and no compensation was offered. Wade has filed a suit against the county to recover his legal costs of $125,000. [The suit was settled out of court in June 1994 for $3.7 million, collected from the city, county, the therapist, and the hospital.]

It is not entirely true, as the slogan maintains, that "nobody wins with child abuse." In this conflict, zealotry can easily forge an alliance with greed. Therapists fight over military referrals backed by the Civilian Health and Medical Program of the Uniformed Services. The program pays nearly double the local rates for therapy: $78.60 for forty-five minutes of therapy. Some therapists charge $1,000 per session on the plethys-mograph, which one practitioner claims can help cure the sexual miscre-ants of the Tailhook scandal through "orgasmic reconditioning."

As Gardner points out, to qualify for federal money under the 1974 Mondale Act, states had to pass legislation that provided immunity from prosecution for all those reporting child abuse. But the system provides no funds for those falsely accused, nor for children used as vehicles of false accusation.

New DNA tests in late December 1992 found a 100 percent match be-tween genetic markers in Carder's blood and the semen evidence in the Wade case. But the DA's office did not press rape charges. Attorney Gen-eral Janet Reno, who made her reputation defending children, might want to investigate.

The grand jury found that, far from being an aberration, there were three hundred cases with elements similar to the Wades'. The Wade case, they wrote, did not even need to be in the system, which was out of control, characterized by secrecy, falsehood, and operating with no effective checks and balances. Wexler's work extends this portrait to the entire nation.

The DA's office justified its handling of the case and defended Via. County Counsel Lloyd Harmon, Via's other boss, maintained that the Wade case "was handled in a thorough and professional manner and with due concern for the rights and interests of all parties." One wonders what an unprofessional case might look like. Perhaps it would resemble that of Dale Akiki, who may well be suffering persecution for his unusual appear-ance and whose case is shaping up as a sequel to the McMartin debacle.

Further abuses

Akiki, thirty-five, suffers from hydrocephalus, which enlarges the head. He also has a concave chest, club feet, woolly hair, and droopy eyelids from Noonan's syndrome, a rare genetic disorder. Akiki's physical diffi-culties include limited use of his elbows. Friends and neighbors portray Akiki as popular, polite, gentle, and particularly dedicated to children.

Akiki and his wife, Gloria, were members of Faith Chapel, a large church near San Diego, where for over a year they oversaw a nursery school on Sunday and Wednesday nights. In 1988, some parents thought that Akiki might be frightening the children, and the church duly re-placed him. Several months later, rumors about indecent exposure began to circulate about Akiki and his wife. Though the stories could not be cor-roborated, the church asked Akiki to leave the congregation and called in the police. Parents began sending children to psychotherapists and the local Center for Child Protection. Most of the children denied that any-thing bad had happened, until they began to undergo "therapy."

It was only after months of these sessions that the children began to claim that they had been dunked underwater, tied up, kicked and punched, urinated on, and subjected to various other atrocities. There was also supposedly animal mutilation and the drinking of blood. Curi-ously, these hideous practices all appear on a checklist widely circulated at therapists' seminars and workshops on ritual abuse. One of the thera-pists and a social worker were coauthors of a hysterical report about ritual abuse, which says that satanic cults are as common as Rotary Clubs and that satanist "breeders" bear children for abuse. The FBI has found no evidence of these vast satanic networks.

Further, Akiki supposedly snuck the children away to a secret house. How he could accomplish all this in the short time when he was watching the children is not clear. Akiki cannot drive a car and has no driver's license.

The Wade case . . . did not even need to be in the system, which was out of control, characterized by secrecy, falsehood, and operating with no effective checks and balances.

In May 1991, Akiki, who has no criminal record, was arrested and has remained in jail ever since. He faces forty-nine counts of child abuse and three of kidnapping that could bring a sentence of three hundred years. [Akiki was acquitted of all charges and was released in November 1993.] A judge denied bail in spite of the fact that virtually every one of the alleged victims recanted their charges and some of the parents have serious doubts. The legal proceedings raise doubts of their own.

Both Kathy Dobbins, the case's first investigator, and initial prosecutor Sally Penso did not believe that there was enough evidence to press charges. Then a prominent San Diego businessman whose three grandchildren were allegedly among Akiki's victims approached District Attorney Edwin Miller, who, like the businessman, is a board member of the Child Abuse Prevention Foundation (CAPF). In fact, the businessman and his company had given the organization some $500,000. Miller promptly booted Penso off the Akiki case and assigned it to prosecutor Mary Avery, a ritual-abuse true believer who is the principal founder of CALF and also a board member. Avery and the wealthy businessman's wife also serve together on the board of the Commission on Children and Youth, another child-abuse organization. It thus appears that Miller allowed a plaintiff to pick his own prosecutor. And there is another fascinating connection in this case.

Harry Elias, now a judge, formerly headed the child-abuse unit. He wanted to put Avery on the case because of its "complexity." Interestingly enough, Elias is married to Kee MacFarlane, whose bogus interviews launched the McMartin debacle and who remains active in child-abuse agencies. *Newsweek* magazine still hails her as an expert.

Such stories are not exclusive to the United States. In January [1993], the London *Spectator* documented a case in which social workers removed a child from his home because the parents were poor. Wexler's *Wounded Innocents* confirms that this also happens in America, where informers remain anonymous and one phone call can still result in a broken family. There are signs, however, that the hysteria may be starting to subside.

In February [1993], a New Jersey court overturned the conviction of Kelly Michaels, a schoolteacher who had been charged with a host of sexual crimes such as raping children with knives and forcing them to drink urine and eat feces. Michaels had been convicted in spite of the fact that there were no witnesses to these crimes and no traces of injury on the children, a situation startlingly similar to the Akiki case. Michaels spent five years in prison and her trial cost $3 million.

In March [1993], the Nevada Supreme Court overturned the conviction of Martha Felix and her nephew Francisco Ontiveros. The case involved allegations of ritual hangings, the drinking of blood, and other atrocities against children. The trial was the longest and costliest in Carson City history, and both defendants had been sentenced to life imprisonment.

In another parentectomy, a San Diego social worker seized the daughter of Gavin O'Hara and placed her in the home of the social worker's sister, who was not a licensed foster parent, for purposes of adoption. The adoption had been discussed, it emerged, before the child had even been born. Social workers told O'Hara that his being a Mormon made it more likely he would abuse his own daughter, roughly equivalent to saying that being Amish makes it likely that one will become an arsonist.

Last November [1992], Wade case veteran Via argued that O'Hara's daughter was suffering "separation anxiety" and should therefore not be returned to her father. Judge Richard Hoffman was having none of it and said that a "dumb system" had "brutalized" the child. He awarded custody to O'Hara and dealt Via a stiff reprimand.

Reining in a runaway system

How could the system be repaired? Columbia's Gardner would like to see the immunity clause dropped and the financial incentive changed. He advocates ending federal funding to states that deprive suspects of due-process protections. But much remains to be done, particularly in oversight.

The social worker in the O'Hara case received only a letter of reprimand for what amounted to a legal kidnapping. There were no dismissals over the Wade case, a shocking miscarriage of justice. It is an open question whether a person who brainwashes a child into falsely accusing her own father of rape should be allowed to practice therapy. But no action has been taken against therapist Kathleen Goodfriend. In fact, she continues to receive lucrative referrals from juvenile court. [In 1996, Goodfriend surrendered her license to practice psychotherapy.]

Also in San Diego, a female social worker was using seized children for child pornography. The woman was not charged, and instead officials allowed her to quietly resign. Investigators believe she may now be working as a social worker in another part of the state.

It would seem fair to judge the child-protection system by its own standard and rhetoric. This is a system that remains in denial. It cannot begin to recover until it recognizes the problem.

4

Repressed Memories of Child Abuse May Be Valid

Minouche Kandel and Eric Kandel

Minouche Kandel is an attorney with the Support Network for Battered Women in Mountain View, California, and a member of the legislative committee of the California Alliance Against Domestic Violence. Eric Kandel is University Professor at Columbia University Center for Neurobiology and Behavior.

In recent decades, a number of adults have uncovered repressed memories of childhood sexual abuse and have confronted their attackers in civil courts. However, a backlash has developed among parents and researchers who maintain that these recovered memories are fabrications. Psychologists dispute whether there is a psychological basis to support the concept of repressed memory. But there may be a biological explanation: In response to trauma, human brains produce natural opiates that block the formation of long-term memory. These blocked memories may later be revived when stress prompts the body to produce adrenaline.

Jennifer H., a professional musician, was 23 when she sought help because she was having problems with sexual intimacy. While in therapy, she also began exploring the unexplained feelings of panic that had haunted her daily since early childhood. Gradually, she says, she traced her feelings of terror to their source, recalling memories she'd repressed since leaving home. She remembered her father first molesting her and then raping her from the time she was 4 until she moved out at 17. She recalled that he had throttled her, threatening to kill her if she told anyone. As these memories resurfaced, her panic attacks and other symptoms receded. But when she confronted her father, a mechanical engineer at a prominent northeastern university, he flatly denied abusing her.

Other family members remembered Jennifer's father grabbing her breasts. Jennifer herself had a memory—never forgotten—of his staring at her chest and making crude sexual remarks. Concerned that her father would abuse other children unless he acknowledged his problem, Jennifer

From Minouche Kandel and Eric Kandel, "Flights of Memory," *Discover*, May 1994, ©1994, Minouche Kandel and Eric Kandel. Reprinted with the permission of *Discover* magazine.

turned to the courts, hoping a lawsuit might prod her father into treatment. The statute of limitations on filing criminal charges had expired, but in 1988 Jennifer brought a personal-injury suit against her father. In addition to her own testimony, the court heard her mother—by then divorced—testify to having seen Jennifer's father lying on top of Jennifer's 14-year-old sister; she also said he'd fondled a baby-sitter in her early teens. Jennifer's father's sister recalled his making sexual passes at young girls. In 1993 a Massachusetts jury ordered him to pay Jennifer $500,000 in damages. (Civil juries can't order people into treatment as part of a judgment.) Although Jennifer's father admitted to fondling the baby-sitter, he maintains to this day that he never abused his daughter.

Until the early 1970s the sexual abuse of children was largely ignored; their stories were doubted and minimized, or they were blamed for encouraging their molestation.

Jennifer H.'s case is one of several recent cases at the heart of a fierce controversy over recovered memories—memories of sexual abuse that come back after a period of repression. It was only in the 1980s that adults who'd been molested as children began to press their claims in court, publicly confronting their abusers in the hope of forcing them to acknowledge their guilt. But as the number of cases has risen, a growing number of parents, researchers, and academics have begun to speak out about the dangers of false accusations. They question in particular whether it's psychologically possible to repress traumatic childhood memories and then recover them. And they suggest that some people, egged on by therapists or self-help books, are fabricating memories of incidents that never occurred. So far, people on both sides of the debate have relied on psychological, rather than biological, insights into how memory works to make their case.

Can biology in fact shed any light on whether and how memories might be repressed and recovered? Perhaps—but to appreciate the debate fully, we first need to put it in its sociological context.

Until the early 1970s the sexual abuse of children was largely ignored; their stories were doubted and minimized, or they were blamed for encouraging their molestation. But research within the past 15 years or so suggests that child molesting is far from rare. Depending on who is asked and how abuse is defined, studies find that between 8 and 38 percent of women say they were abused as children, while figures for men range from 3 to 16 percent. (The 38 percent figure is from a random survey in 1978 of 930 women in San Francisco that defined abuse as any unwanted sexual activity with a relative before age 18; fondling, rape, or attempted rape by a nonrelative of children under 14; and attempted or completed forcible rape by a nonrelative of children ages 14 to 17—descriptions consistent with criminal law definitions of child molestation.)

Many adults who were abused as children clearly remember the experience all too well. But studies by Harvard psychiatrist Judith Herman and others also suggest that temporarily repressing such memories may not be uncommon. In 1987 Herman found that of 53 women attending incest survivor groups, almost two-thirds reported partial or complete memory lapses at some point after the abuse occurred. These findings have since been echoed in a larger survey of men as well as women led by psychiatrist John Briere at the University of Southern California School of Medicine. The earlier the abuse occurred, and the more violent or persistent it was, the more likely victims were to block the memory for long periods—a finding that gels with the clinical studies of Lenore Terr, a psychiatrist at the University of California at San Francisco, who finds that children exposed to repeated traumas are more likely to repress them than children suffering a one-time traumatic event.

One of the most systematic efforts to track memory repression was conducted by Linda Meyer Williams, a sociologist at the University of New Hampshire. Williams interviewed 129 women who were treated for sexual abuse when they were young girls in the mid-1970s. More than one-third had no memory of, or chose not to report, the molestation documented in their medical records. Since over half of these women discussed other incidents of sexual abuse, selective amnesia is a more likely explanation for their response (or lack of it) than any unwillingness to discuss sex.

Most clinical psychologists believe that children can learn to block memories as a survival mechanism: if physical escape from their tormentors is impossible, psychological escape may become crucial. When children can't avoid abuse and know it's going to be repeated, some cope by tuning out—mentally dissociating themselves from the abuse while it's occurring—or by repressing the memory afterward.

But repression, according to this school of thought, may cease to be helpful in adult life. Away from the traumatic environment, adults may find their memories resurfacing, either gradually in fragments, or suddenly in vivid flashbacks. As in Jennifer H.'s case, these memories may return during therapy, but that's by no means always the case. Frank Fitzpatrick was 38, married, and securely employed as an insurance adjuster in Rhode Island when he spontaneously recalled being molested by Father James Porter 26 years earlier. Since being confronted by Fitzpatrick in 1990, the Roman Catholic priest has admitted to molesting dozens of boys and girls. When the news became public, 68 men and women said that they too had been assaulted by Father Porter. At least half a dozen recalled the abuse only after news reports triggered the return of their childhood memories.

True and false memories in criminal accusations

But people accused of abuse don't often confess—and their accusers' stories can't easily be corroborated. That leaves memory as the basis of many criminal and civil cases and makes determining the accuracy of people's memories of paramount importance. Because child molestation is so abhorrent, the mere taint of suspicion can ruin lives. Those accused risk losing their families, careers, and reputations; they face high legal costs and potentially prison if criminal charges are pressed. According to the False Memory Syndrome Foundation, over 9,500 U.S. families now claim that their adult children have tarred them with abuses that never occurred. (The foundation was established in 1992 by Pamela and Peter Freyd after their daughter Jennifer, now a professor of psychology at the University of Oregon, confronted them with accusations of abuse by her father—an allegation they have energetically disputed.) Many of these families blame zealous therapists and popular self-help books for encouraging their children's "fake memories."

That false memories occur and that some people are unjustly accused can't be denied, but . . . skeptics seize on such cases to cast doubt on all *repressed memories.*

Some researchers—among them psychologists Elizabeth Loftus of the University of Washington and Richard Ofshe of the University of California at Berkeley—have joined them in casting doubt on the believability of repressed memories. Publicity about child abuse, they argue, has fostered a climate in which it's all too tempting to believe that hidden abuse is the cause of many people's ill-defined symptoms of distress.

Loftus and Ofshe think that, consciously or carelessly, some therapists are seeding ideas into vulnerable patients' minds. Fictitious memories, they point out, can be implanted with hypnosis—or even without. Loftus cites a study in which five people were told a false story by an older relative about how they'd gotten lost in a mall or apartment complex as children. When they were later asked to recall further details, they related elaborate memories of the fictitious incident. Is it as easy to implant something as traumatic as being repeatedly raped by someone in your family? There may indeed be powerful disincentives to admitting to false memories. Nevertheless it's still striking how very few cases come to light.

As further evidence of the malleability of memory, Loftus and Ofshe cite the sensational case of Paul Ingram, a deputy sheriff in Washington State whose two daughters accused him of sexually abusing them as part of a Satanic cult. Ingram, a fundamentalist Christian, denied the charge. In jail, though, he was repeatedly questioned about the alleged incidents by the police and a minister, and was asked to visualize them by a psychologist—until he finally came up with lurid memories of the incidents. Ofshe was originally hired to interview Ingram by the prosecution, not the defense. To test Ingram's suggestibility, Ofshe asked him about a scene—entirely invented—in which Ingram forced his son and daughter to have sex. At first Ingram recalled nothing. Then Ofshe encouraged Ingram to imagine the scene and to "pray on the image," as Ingram had done before. Ingram subsequently developed detailed memories about the invented scenario, casting doubt on all of his previous confessions.

The Ingram case suggests some conditions that might facilitate the creation of entirely false memories: institutionalization or religious pressure. Of ten "recanters" whose cases have come to light, one woman acquired her memories of abuse in the isolation unit of a private hospital. Another was hospitalized in a program run by a Christian organization. Two other recanters have accused their therapists of using powerful psychotropic drugs, which, like hypnosis, can increase susceptibility to suggestion. That false memories occur and that some people are unjustly accused can't be denied, but Ofshe and other skeptics seize on such cases to cast doubt on *all* repressed memories.

In a 1993 article in *Society*, Ofshe concludes: "Only pre-therapy accounts of a person's history can be treated as a normal memory with only the ordinary component of error." In his view memory repression is no more than "unsubstantiated speculation."

What, then, can biology contribute to this difficult debate? Over the past 20 years neuroscientists have made considerable strides in understanding the workings of memory. Can science also explain the delayed recall of sexual trauma? The *rigorous* answer is no. There is, as yet, no proper understanding of what might happen in human brains when memories are repressed, or when they are recovered. However, biology *can* provide insights into how a memory is stored, how that storage is regulated, and whether this regulation is compatible with repression and with a later return of memory.

Neurological mechanisms of memory formation

What are the cellular mechanisms that explain how memories are created? As far as we know, storing our experiences as memories involves altering the strength of connections—known as synapses—between nerve cells in the brain. In its initial phase, which lasts minutes and is commonly called short-term memory, the change is temporary; it doesn't alter the structure of the connections. One or more hours later, though, anatomical changes begin to convert the memory into a longer-lasting form. This consolidation period involves the growth of new connections between nerve cells, or in some cases, the retraction of existing connections.

We also know that both short-term and long-term memories consist of at least two distinct forms: implicit and explicit. Implicit memory deals with our unconscious knowledge of motor or perceptual skills, or "knowing how." Explicit memory deals with our knowledge of facts, people, and places, or "knowing that." Quite different brain systems participate in storing these two forms. Explicit memory is handled by the inside segments of the temporal lobes (the brain lobes located behind our ears) and an underlying region called the hippocampus. Implicit memory, in contrast, involves distinct motor or sensory pathways in the brain, the autonomic nervous system (which regulates involuntary actions such as breathing and heart rate), and two additional brain structures called the amygdala and the cerebellum.

The first evidence that the temporal lobes and hippocampus play a role in explicit memory came in the 1950s from studies of epileptic patients. Brenda Milner, a neuropsychologist at the Montreal Neurological Institute, described the now famous case of H.M., a 27-year-old assembly-line worker who suffered from uncontrollable temporal lobe seizures. To alleviate his seizures, a surgeon removed parts of his temporal lobe, including the hippocampus. This operation left H.M. with a devastating memory deficit: he could no longer form *new* long-term memories. Yet H.M. still had his store of previously acquired long-term memories. He remembered well events before his surgery, such as his job and his childhood experiences. From the study of H.M. and patients like him, it became apparent that the hippocampus is only an interim depository for long-term memory. The hippocampus processes the newly learned information for a period of weeks to months, then transfers the information up to the cerebral cortex for more permanent storage. Thus, although H.M. still had a perfectly intact short-term memory, he couldn't translate what he learned into long-term memory. He could converse normally with Milner every time he saw her, but he could not remember her from visit to visit.

At first it was thought that this shattering deficit applied to all forms of new learning. But Milner and others soon made a wonderful discovery that revolutionized thinking about memory. Patients with temporal lobe lesions *can* accomplish certain implicit types of learning tasks involving perceptual and motor skill —and they retain the memory of these tasks perfectly well. H.M., for example, could learn new motor skills, such as mirror drawing (drawing while looking at his hand in a mirror, rather than looking at the paper). Usually there's cross talk between the explicit and implicit memory systems, so that when you learn or experience something new, both systems come into play. In fact, some types of explicit memory can be transformed into implicit memory by constant repetition. Learning to hit a backhand in tennis at first involves deliberate, conscious thought, but hitting good ground strokes becomes almost reflexive with practice. You don't consciously recall what to do—you just know what hitting a backhand *feels* like.

If an incident is so distressing that the brain makes opiates to dull the pain, the opiates may interfere with the memory-storing process.

This cross talk is particularly evident in memories of emotionally charged experiences such as sexual abuse, in which the emotion associated with the event and the conscious recollection of the event are stored in separate systems. Much of what we know about "emotional memory" comes from work done by neuroscientists Joseph LeDoux at New York University and Michael Davis at Yale. These studies indicate that the conscious component of highly charged memories is initially stored in the hippocampus. But the unconscious, implicit component is probably stored through the amygdala, which links the brain's sensory and motor areas to the autonomic nervous system. In memories of very stressful events, the role of implicit memory may be particularly powerful.

Of course, like all memories, highly charged memories need a period of consolidation to become long-term. But Michela Gallagher at the University of North Carolina and others who study this process have found out something very interesting: the *strength* of long-term memory can be affected by the context in which the remembered event occurs. Some factors enhance memory consolidation, storage, and recall; others inhibit them.

Working with rats, Gallagher has found that implicit memories of fearful experiences are strengthened when noradrenaline—a neurotransmitter associated with alertness and stress—is released in the amygdala. In contrast, the release of naturally occurring opiumlike substances, called endogenous opiates, weakens memory storage. Other researchers have since found that explicit aspects of fear can be similarly modulated. This finding suggests a fascinating possibility. If an incident is so distressing that the brain makes opiates to dull the pain, the opiates may interfere with the memory-storing process. Intriguingly, Gallagher finds that using a drug called nalaxone to block endogenous opiates at the time of consolidation *does* enhance memory recall in rats. Furthermore, some studies show that a weakly stored memory can be enhanced by injecting a stimulant drug like adrenaline.

Such studies give us a biological context for considering how traumatic memories might be suppressed in humans, but what about their retrieval? We can only speculate about how this might work.

Let's suppose that a memory is stored weakly in the explicit system because endogenous opiates interfered with its consolidation—so weakly that the person has no conscious memory of the original wrenching event. That same event, though, might also be captured by the implicit system through a characteristic physical sensation or gesture. Perhaps later the implicit system may provide clues—such as physical sensations—that help stir the recall of weak explicit memories.

In fact, people who say they were abused as children often *do* describe their memories returning first as bodily sensations: Jennifer H. was doing exercises to relieve the tension in her neck when she recalled her father's choking her. Sometimes, says Lenore Terr, a victim shows behavioral clues that reflect the traumatic event. Terr cites the case of Eileen Franklin, who said she saw her father rape her best friend and crush the girl's head with a rock. The father was also abusing Franklin, who was 8 at the time. From age 8 to 14, Franklin pulled out the hair from a particular part of her scalp until it bled, re-creating the wound she'd seen inflicted on her friend. Franklin repressed the memory until she was in her late twenties, when its resurgence resulted in her father's conviction.

Indeed, some survivors of abuse describe their recovered memories as qualitatively different from other memories: they feel as if they're actually reexperiencing the event, with all its textures, smells, and physical sensations. This parallels the intensity of flashbacks experienced by combat veterans. As we have seen, Gallagher found that implicit memory can be strengthened by stimulating noradrenaline in the amygdala. And studies at Yale have suggested that noradrenaline released in response to stress contributes to the powerful flashbacks of Vietnam veterans. Perhaps memories that sexual abuse survivors are normally unable to access are retrieved when their noradrenaline system is activated.

A neurological basis for repressed memories

All this suggests that the action of endogenous opiates and noradrenaline in the amygdala and hippocampus could begin to provide a biological framework for examining how memories are repressed and later retrieved. It may soon be feasible to examine these ideas directly. Animal studies have already shown that the signature of long-term memory, both implicit and explicit, is anatomical change—the growth or retraction of connections between nerve cells in the brain. Improvements in brain imaging (such as magnetic resonance imaging) may eventually let us examine even small structures in the human brain in a safe, noninvasive way. We may then be able to see whether sexual abuse leads to physical changes in the amygdala that reflect a person's memories of the event—and whether these changes can be modulated by the noradrenergic and opioid systems.

Indeed, existing imaging techniques—PET scans—have already let us glimpse why false memories might seem entirely real to those who experience them. Stephen Kosslyn at Harvard has found that the brain area involved in *perceiving* an image and storing it as a memory is also involved in *imagining* that image. For example, when you think about the face of a person you met yesterday, the medial temporal region—the very same region used to perceive that face in the first place—becomes active. Thus an imagined event might be mistaken for a perceived event since both use the same brain architecture. In fact, in many ways memory *is* like perception. Both are reconstructed events in the brain, creative elaborations that involve filling in details around a few solid visual landmarks. Much as the fine points of perception are fallible to illusion, the details of memory are fallible to suggestion.

In reality, given the private nature of child abuse and the threats made to children to prevent them from telling others, independent evidence often isn't available.

Thus, viewed from a biological perspective, there's reason to believe that both sides of the repressed memory debate can be valid. Research in animals suggests that memory storage *can* be modulated and inhibited, and that once inhibited, memory can nevertheless return. At the same time, we also know that memory can be unreliable and we have an inkling of how fantasy might be mistaken for reality. How, then, to evaluate—right now—the data from any individual case? The answer is clear: ideally, one wants to see independent evidence to corroborate the putative victim's report—for instance, from family members, diaries, photographs, medical and police records. But in reality, given the private nature of child abuse and the threats made to children to prevent them from telling others, independent evidence often isn't available. (Failing independent corroboration, particularly compelling behavioral clues, like those displayed by Eileen Franklin, might sometimes help support a case.)

So the arguments continue. But what's disturbing about the current tone of the debate is the eagerness with which some media and academic critics are using the wedge of doubt to publicly discredit the very existence of delayed memories. Do the questions of the critics reflect a genuine effort to get at the truth, to defend the innocence of the wrongfully accused? Or are we sometimes witnessing a backlash against the struggle to bring child abuse out of the family closet? At an American Psychiatric Association meeting in 1993, Herman noted: "Until recently the sexual abuse of children was the perfect crime. The perpetrator was fairly guaranteed that he would never be caught or successfully prosecuted. Now women—and men—have begun to use the courts to hold them accountable for the first time, and we see the perpetrators fighting back."

5

Recovered Memories of Child Abuse Are Unreliable

Elizabeth Loftus

Elizabeth Loftus is a professor of psychology at the University of Washington in Seattle. She is the coauthor of The Myth of Repressed Memory.

Modern-day accusations of child sexual abuse by adults who have supposedly uncovered memories of childhood molestation are analogous to the witch hunts of the sixteenth and seventeenth centuries. Like the "witches" of the past, parents and child-care workers today are often convicted of the most heinous acts with only the word of their accusers offered as evidence. Recovered memories of childhood molestation are often the product of suggestion by overzealous and ill-trained psychotherapists. Reform within the profession of psychotherapy is needed to end the production of false accusations of child abuse.

We live in a strange and precarious time that resembles at its heart the hysteria and superstitious fervor of the witch trials of the sixteenth and seventeenth centuries. Men and women are being accused, tried, and convicted with no proof or evidence of guilt other than the word of the accuser. Even when the accusations involve numerous perpetrators, inflicting grievous wounds over many years, even decades, the accuser's pointing finger of blame is enough to make believers of judges and juries. Individuals are being imprisoned on the "evidence" provided by memories that come back in dreams and flashbacks—memories that did not exist until a person wandered into therapy and was asked point-blank, "Were you ever sexually abused as a child?" And then begins the process of excavating the "repressed" memories through invasive therapeutic techniques, such as age regression, guided visualization, trance writing, dream work, body work, and hypnosis.

One case that seems to fit the mold led to highly bizarre satanic-abuse memories. An account of the case is described in detail by one of the expert witnesses (Rogers 1992) and is briefly reviewed by Loftus and Ketcham (1994).

From Elizabeth Loftus, "Remembering Dangerously," *Skeptical Inquirer*, March/April 1995. Reprinted by permission of the Committee for the Scientific Investigation of Claims of the Paranormal.

A woman in her mid-seventies and her recently deceased husband were accused by their two adult daughters of rape, sodomy, forced oral sex, torture by electric shock, and the ritualistic murder of babies. The older daughter, 48 years old at the time of the lawsuit, testified that she was abused from infancy until age 25. The younger daughter alleged abuse from infancy to age 15. A granddaughter also claimed that she was abused by her grandmother from infancy to age 8.

The memories were recovered when the adult daughters went into therapy in 1987 and 1988. After the breakup of her third marriage, the older daughter started psychotherapy, eventually diagnosing herself as a victim of multiple-personality disorder and satanic ritual abuse. She convinced her sister and her niece to begin therapy and joined in their therapy sessions for the first year. The two sisters also attended group therapy with other multiple-personality-disorder patients who claimed to be victims of satanic ritual abuse.

For long sections of the tape it was hard to tell who was the patient and who was the therapist.

In therapy the older sister recalled a horrifying incident that occurred when she was four or five years old. Her mother caught a rabbit, chopped off one of its ears, smeared the blood over her body, and then handed the knife to her, expecting her to kill the animal. When she refused, her mother poured scalding water over her arms. When she was 13 and her sister was still in diapers, a group of Satanists demanded that the sisters disembowel a dog with a knife. She remembered being forced to watch as a man who threatened to divulge the secrets of the cult was burned with a torch. Other members of the cult were subjected to electric shocks in rituals that took place in a cave. The cult even made her murder her own newborn baby. When asked for more details about these horrific events, she testified in court that her memory was impaired because she was frequently drugged by the cult members.

The younger sister remembered being molested on a piano bench by her father while his friends watched. She recalled being impregnated by members of the cult at ages 14 and 16, and both pregnancies were ritually aborted. She remembered one incident in the library where she had to eat a jar of pus and another jar of scabs. Her daughter remembered seeing her grandmother in a black robe carrying a candle and being drugged on two occasions and forced to ride in a limousine with several prostitutes.

The jury found the accused woman guilty of neglect. It did not find any intent to harm and thus refused to award monetary damages. Attempts to appeal the decision have failed.

Are the women's memories authentic? The "infancy" memories are almost certainly false memories given the scientific literature on childhood amnesia. Moreover, no evidence in the form of bones or dead bodies was ever produced that might have corroborated the human-sacrifice memories. If these memories are indeed false, as they appear to be, where would they come from? George Ganaway, a clinical assistant professor of psychiatry at the Emory University School of Medicine, has proposed that unwitting suggestions from therapy play an important role in the development of false satanic memories.

What goes on in therapy?

Since therapy is done in private, it is not particularly easy to find out what really goes on behind that closed door. But there are clues that can be derived from various sources. Therapists' accounts, patients' accounts, and sworn statements from litigation have revealed that highly suggestive techniques go on in some therapists' offices (Lindsay and Read 1994; Loftus 1993; Yapko 1994).

Other evidence of misguided if not reckless beliefs and practices comes from several cases in which private investigators, posing as patients, have gone undercover into therapists' offices. In one case, the pseudopatient visited the therapist complaining about nightmares and trouble sleeping. On the third visit to the therapist, the investigator was told that she was an incest survivor (Loftus 1993). In another case, Cable News Network (CNN 1993) sent an employee undercover to the offices of an Ohio psychotherapist (who was supervised by a psychologist) wired with a hidden video camera. The pseudopatient complained of feeling depressed and having recent relationship problems with her husband. In the first session, the therapist diagnosed "incest survivor," telling the pseudopatient she was a "classic case." When the pseudopatient returned for her second session, puzzled about her lack of memory, the therapist told her that her reaction was typical and that she had repressed the memory because the trauma was so awful. A third case, based on surreptitious recordings of a therapist from the southwestern region of the United States, was inspired by the previous efforts.

Inside a southwestern therapist's office

In the summer of 1993, a woman (call her "Willa") had a serious problem. Her older sister, a struggling artist, had a dream that she reported to her therapist. The dream got interpreted as evidence of a history of sexual abuse. Ultimately the sister confronted the parents in a videotaped session at the therapist's office. The parents were mortified; the family was wrenched irreparably apart.

Willa tried desperately to find out more about the sister's therapy. On her own initiative, Willa hired a private investigator to pose as a patient and seek therapy from the sister's therapist. The private investigator called herself Ruth. She twice visited the therapist, an M.A. in counseling and guidance who was supervised by a Ph.D., and secretly tape-recorded both of the sessions.

In the first session, Ruth told the therapist that she had been rear-ended in an auto accident a few months earlier and was having trouble getting over it. Ruth said that she would just sit for weeks and cry for no apparent reason. The therapist seemed totally disinterested in getting any history regarding the accident, but instead wanted to talk about Ruth's childhood. While discussing her early life, Ruth volunteered a recurring dream that she had had in childhood and said the dream had now returned. In the dream she is 4 or 5 years old and there is a massive white bull after her that catches her and gores her somewhere in the upper thigh area, leaving her covered with blood.

The therapist decided that the stress and sadness that Ruth was currently experiencing was tied to her childhood, since she'd had the same dream as a child. She decided the "night terrors" (as she called them) were evidence that Ruth was suffering from post-traumatic-stress disorder (PTSD). They would use guided imagery to find the source of the childhood trauma. Before actually launching this approach, the therapist informed her patient that she, the therapist, was an incest survivor: "I was incested by my grandfather."

That these kinds of activities can and do sometimes lead to false memories seems now to be beyond dispute.

During the guided imagery, Ruth was asked to imagine herself as a little child. She then talked about the trauma of her parents' divorce and of her father's remarriage to a younger woman who resembled Ruth herself. The therapist wanted to know if Ruth's father had had affairs, and she told Ruth that hers had, and that this was a "generational" thing that came from the grandfathers. The therapist led Ruth through confusing/suggestive/manipulative imagery involving a man holding down a little girl somewhere in a bedroom. The therapist decided that Ruth was suffering from a "major grief issue" and told her it was sexual: "I don't think, with the imagery and his marrying someone who looks like you, that it could be anything else."

The second session, two days later, began:

> Pseudopatient: You think I am quite possibly a victim of sexual abuse?

> Therapist: Um-huh. Quite possibly. It's how I would put it. You know, you don't have the real definitive data that says that, but, um, the first thing that made me think about that was the blood on your thighs. You know, I just wonder, like where would that come from in a child's reality. And, um, the fact that in the imagery the child took you or the child showed you the bedroom and your father holding you down in the bedroom . . . it would be really hard for me to think otherwise. . . . Something would have to come up in your work to really prove that it really wasn't about sexual abuse.

Ruth said she had no memory of such abuse but that didn't dissuade the therapist for a minute.

> Pseudopatient: . . . I can remember a lot of anger and fear associated with him, but I can't recall physical sexual abuse. Do people always remember?

> Therapist: No. . . . Hardly ever. . . . It happened to you a long

time ago and your body holds on to the memory and that's why being in something like a car accident might trigger memories. . . .

The therapist shared her own experiences of abuse, now by her father, which supposedly led to anorexia, bulimia, overspending, excessive drinking, and other destructive behaviors from which the therapist had presumably now recovered. For long sections of the tape it was hard to tell who was the patient and who was the therapist.

Later the therapist offered these bits of wisdom:

> I don't know how many people I think are really in psychiatric hospitals who are really just incest survivors or, um, have repressed memories.

> It will be a grief issue that your father was—sexualized you—and was not an appropriate father.

> You need to take that image of yourself as an infant, with the hand over, somebody's trying to stifle your crying, and feeling pain somewhere as a memory.

The therapist encouraged Ruth to read two books: *The Courage to Heal*, which she called the "bible of healing from childhood sexual abuse," and the workbook that goes with it. She made a special point of talking about the section on confrontation with the perpetrator. Confrontation, she said, wasn't necessarily for everyone. Some don't want to do it if it will jeopardize their inheritance, in which case, the therapist said, you can do it after the person is dead—you can do eulogies. But confrontation is empowering, she told Ruth.

Then to Ruth's surprise, the therapist described the recent confrontation she had done with Willa's sister (providing sufficient detail about the unnamed patient that there could be little doubt about who it was).

> Therapist: I just worked with someone who did do it with her parents. Called both of her parents in and we did it in here. . . . It's empowering because you're stepping out on your own. She said she felt like she was 21, and going out on her own for the first time, you know, that's what she felt like. . . .

> Pseudopatient: And, did her parents deny or—

> Therapist: Oh, they certainly did—

> Pseudopatient: Did she remember, that she—she wasn't groping like me?

> Therapist: She groped a lot in the beginning. But it sort of, you know, just like pieces of a puzzle, you know, you start to get them and then eventually you can make a picture with it. And she was able to do that. And memory is a funny thing. It's not always really accurate in terms of ages, and

times and places and that kind of thing. Like you may have any variable superimposed on another. Like I have a friend who had an ongoing sexual abuse and she would have a memory of, say, being on this couch when she was seven and being abused there, but they didn't have that couch when she was seven, they had it when she was five. . . . It doesn't discount the memory, it just means that it probably went on more than once and so those memories overlap. . . .

Pseudopatient: This woman who did the confrontation, is she free now? Does she feel freed over it?

Therapist: Well, she doesn't feel free from her history . . . but she does feel like she owns it now and it doesn't own her . . . and she has gotten another memory since the confrontation. . . .

The therapist told Ruth all about the "new memory" of her other patient, Willa's sister:

Therapist: [It was in] the early-morning hours and she was just lying awake, and she started just having this feeling of, it was like her hands became uncontrollable and it was like she was masturbating someone. She was like going faster than she could have, even in real life, so that she knew, it was familiar enough to her as it will be to you, that she knew what it was, and it really did not freak her out at all. . . . She knew there was a memory there she was sitting on.

Before Ruth's second therapy session had ended, Ruth's mother was brought into the picture—guilty, at least, of betrayal by neglect:

Therapist: Well, you don't have to have rational reasons, either, to feel betrayed. The only thing that a child needs to feel is that there was probably a part of you that was just yearning for your mother and that she wasn't there. And whether she wasn't there because she didn't know and was off doing something else, or whether she was there and she knew and she didn't do anything about it. It doesn't matter. All the child knew was that Mom wasn't there. And, in that way she was betrayed, you know, whether it was through imperfection on your mother's part or not, and you have to give yourself permission to feel that way without justification, or without rationalization because you were.

Ruth tried again to broach the subject of imagination versus memory:

Pseudopatient: How do we know, when the memories come, what are symbols, that it's not our imagination or something?

Therapist: Why would you image this, of all things. If it were your imagination, you'd be imaging how warm and loving he was. . . . I have a therapist friend who says that the

only proof she needs to know that something happened is
if you think it might have.

At the doorway as Ruth was leaving, her therapist asked if she could
hug her, then did so while telling Ruth how brave she was. A few weeks
later, Ruth got a bill. She was charged $65 for each session.

Rabinowitz (1993) put it well: "The beauty of the repressed incest explanation is that, to enjoy its victim benefits, and the distinction of being associated with a survivor group, it isn't even necessary to have any
recollection that such abuse took place." Actually, being a victim of abuse
without any memories does not sit well, especially when group therapy
comes into play and women without memories interact with those who
do have memories. The pressure to find memories can be very great.

Chu (1992: 7) pointed out one of the dangers of pursuing a fruitless
search (for memories): it masks the real issues from therapeutic exploration. Sometimes patients produce "ever more grotesque and increasingly unbelievable stories in an effort to discredit the material and break
the cycle. Unfortunately, some therapists can't take the hint!"

The southwestern therapist who treated Ruth diagnosed sexual trauma
in the first session. She pursued her sex-abuse agenda in the questions she
asked, in the answers she interpreted, in the way she discussed dreams, in
the books she recommended. An important question remains as to how
common these activities might be. Some clinicians would like to believe
that the problem of overzealous psychotherapists is on a "very small" scale
(Cronin 1994: 31). A recent survey of doctoral-level psychologists indicates
that as many as a quarter may harbor beliefs and engage in practices that
are questionable (Poole and Lindsay 1994). That these kinds of activities can
and do sometimes lead to false memories seems now to be beyond dispute
(Goldstein and Farmer 1993). That these kinds of activities can create false
victims, as well as hurt true ones, also seems now to be beyond dispute.

The place of repressed memories in modern society

Why at this time in our society is there such an interest in "repression"
and the uncovering of repressed memories? Why is it that almost everyone you talk to either knows someone with a "repressed memory" or
knows someone who's being accused, or is just plain interested in the issue? Why do so many individuals believe these stories, even the more
bizarre, outlandish, and outrageous ones? Why is the cry of "witch hunt"
now so loud (Baker 1992: 48; Gardner 1991)? *Witch hunt* is, of course, a
term that gets used by lots of people who have been faced by a pack of accusers (Watson 1992).

"Witch hunt" stems from an analogy between the current allegations
and the witch-craze of the sixteenth and seventeenth centuries, an analog that several analysts have drawn (McHugh 1992; Trott 1991; Victor
1991). As the preeminent British historian Hugh Trevor-Roper (1967) has
noted, the European witch-craze was a perplexing phenomenon. By some
estimates, a half-million people were convicted of witchcraft and burned
to death in Europe alone between the fifteenth and seventeenth centuries
(Harris 1974: 207–258). How did this happen?

It is a dazzling experience to step back in time, as Trevor-Roper guides his readers, first to the eighth century, when the belief in witches was thought to be "unchristian" and in some places the death penalty was decreed for anyone who burnt supposed witches. In the ninth century, almost no one believed that witches could make bad weather, and almost everyone believed that night-flying was a hallucination. But by the beginning of the sixteenth century, there was a complete reversal of these views. "The monks of the late Middle Ages sowed; the lawyers of the sixteenth century reaped; and what a harvest of witches they gathered in!" (Trevor-Roper 1967: 93). Countries that had never known witches were now found to be swarming with them. Thousands of old women (and some young ones) began confessing to being witches who had made secret pacts with the Devil. At night, they said, they anointed themselves with "devil's grease" (made from the fat of murdered infants), and thus lubricated they slipped up chimneys, mounted broomsticks, and flew off on long journeys to a rendezvous called the witches' sabbat. Once they reached the sabbat, they saw their friends and neighbors all worshipping the Devil himself. The Devil sometimes appeared as a big, black, bearded man, sometimes as a stinking goat, and sometimes as a great toad. However he looked, the witches threw themselves into promiscuous sexual orgies with him. While the story might vary from witch to witch, at the core was the Devil, and the witches were thought to be his earth agents in the struggle for control of the spiritual world.

Throughout the sixteenth century, people believed in the general theory, even if they did not accept all of the esoteric details. For two centuries, the clergy preached against the witches. Lawyers sentenced them. Books and sermons warned of their danger. Torture was used to extract confessions. The agents of Satan were soon found to be everywhere. Skeptics, whether in universities, in judges' seats, or on the royal throne, were denounced as witches themselves, and joined the old women at the burning stake. In the absence of physical evidence (such as a pot full of human limbs, or a written pact with the Devil), circumstantial evidence was sufficient. Such evidence did not need to be very cogent (a wart, an insensitive spot that did not bleed when pricked, a capacity to float when thrown in water, an incapacity to shed tears, a tendency to look down when accused). Any of these "indicia" might justify the use of torture to produce a confession (which was proof) or the refusal to confess (which was also proof) and justified even more ferocious tortures and ultimately death.

When did it end? In the middle of the seventeenth century the basis of the craze began to dissolve. As Trevor-Roper (1967: 97) put it, "The rubbish of the human mind, which for two centuries, by some process of intellectual alchemy and social pressure, had become fused together in a coherent, explosive system, has disintegrated. It is rubbish again."

Scapegoating by the church

Various interpretations of this period in social history can be found. Trevor-Roper argued that during periods of intolerance any society looks for scapegoats. For the Catholic church of that period, and in particular their most active members, the Dominicans, the witches were perfect as scapegoats; and so, with relentless propaganda, they created a hatred of witches. The first individuals to be so labeled were the innocently nonconforming social groups. Sometimes they were induced to confess by torture too terrible to bear (e.g., the "leg screw" squeezed the calf and broke the shinbone in pieces; the "lift" hoisted the arms fiercely behind and back; the "ram" or "witch-chair" provided a heated seat of spikes for the witch to sit on). But sometimes confessions came about spontaneously, making their truth even more convincing to others. Gradually laws changed to meet the growth of witches—including laws permitting judicial torture.

There is today a "great fear" that grips our society, and that is fear of child abuse.

There were skeptics, but many of them did not survive. Generally they tried to question the plausibility of the confessions, or the efficacy of torture, or the identification of particular witches. They had little impact, Trevor-Roper claims, because they danced around the edges rather than tackling the core: the concept of Satan. With the mythology intact, it creates its own evidence that is very difficult to disprove. So how did the mythology that had lasted for two centuries lose its force? Finally, challenges against the whole idea of Satan's kingdom were launched. The stereotype of the witch would soon be gone, but not before tens of thousands of witches had been burned or hanged, or both (Watson 1992).

Trevor-Roper saw the witch-craze as a social movement, but with individual extensions. Witch accusations could be used to destroy powerful enemies or dangerous persons. When a "great fear" grips a society, that society looks to the stereotype of the enemy in its midst and points the finger of accusation. In times of panic, he argued, the persecution extends from the weak (the old women who were ordinarily the victims of village hatred) to the strong (the educated judges and derby who resisted the craze). One indicia of "great fear" is when the elite of society are accused of being in league with the enemies.

Is it fair to compare the modern cases of "de-repressed memory" of child sexual trauma to the witch-crazes of several centuries ago? There are some parallels, but the differences are just as striking. In terms of similarities, some of the modern stories actually resemble the stories of earlier times (e.g., witches flying into bedrooms). Sometimes the stories encompass past-life memories (Stevenson 1994) or take on an even more bizarre, alien twist (Mack 1994).[1] In terms of differences, take a look at the accused and the accusers. In the most infamous witch hunt in North America, 300 years ago in Salem, Massachusetts, three-fourths of the accused were women (Watson 1992). Today, they are predominantly (but not all) men. Witches in New England were mostly poor women over 40 who were misfits, although later the set of witches included men (often the witches' husbands or sons), and still later the set expanded to include clergy, prominent merchants, or anyone who had dared to make an enemy. Today, the accused are often men of power and success. The witch accusations of past times were more often leveled by men, but today the accusations are predominantly leveled by women. Today's phenomenon is more than anything a movement of the weak against the strong. There is today a "great fear" that grips our society, and that is fear of child abuse. Rightfully we wish to ferret out these genuine "enemies" and point every finger of accusation at them. But this does not mean, of course, that every perceived enemy, every person with whom we may have feuded, should be labeled in this same way.

Trevor-Roper persuasively argued that the skeptics during the witch-craze did not make much of a dent in the frequency of bonfires and burnings until they challenged the core belief in Satan. What is the analog to that core today? It may be some of the widely cherished beliefs of psychotherapists, such as the belief in the repressed-memory folklore. The repression theory is well articulated by Steele (1994: 41). It is the theory "that we forget events because they are too horrible to contemplate; that we cannot remember these forgotten events by any normal process of casting our minds back but can reliably retrieve them by special techniques; that these forgotten events, banished from consciousness, strive to enter it in disguised forms; that forgotten events have the power to cause apparently unrelated problems in our lives, which can be cured by excavating and reliving the forgotten event."

Is it time to admit that the repression folklore is simply a fairy tale? The tale may be appealing, but what of its relationship to science? Unfortunately, it is partly refuted, partly untested, and partly untestable. This is not to say that all recovered memories are thus false. Responsible skepticism is skepticism about some claims of recovered memory. It is not blanket rejection of all claims. People sometimes remember what was once forgotten; such forgetting and remembering does not mean repression and de-repression, but it does mean that some recently remembered events might reflect authentic memories. Each case must be examined on its merits to explore the credibility, the timing, the motives, the potential for suggestion, the corroboration, and other features to make an intelligent assessment of what any mental product means.

The case of Jennifer H.

Some writers have offered individual cases as proof that a stream of traumas can be massively repressed. Readers must beware that these case "proofs" may leave out critical information. Consider the supposedly ironclad case of Jennifer H. offered by Kandel and Kandel (1994) to readers of *Discover* magazine as an example of a corroborated de-repressed memory. According to the *Discover* account, Jennifer was a 23-year-old musician who recovered memories in therapy of her father raping her from the time she was 4 until she was 17. As her memories resurfaced, her panic attacks and other symptoms receded. Her father, a mechanical-engineering professor, denied any abuse. According to the *Discover* account, Jennifer sued her father, and at trial "corroboration" was produced: Jennifer's mother testified that she had seen the father lying on top of Jennifer's 14-year-old sister and that he had once fondled a baby-sitter in her early teens. The defendant's sister recalled his making passes at young girls. Before this case becomes urban legend and is used as proof of something that it might not be proof of, readers are entitled to know more.

Jennifer's case against her father went to trial in June 1993 in the U.S. District Court for the District of Massachusetts (*Hoult* v. *Hoult*, 1993). The case received considerable media attention (e.g., Kessler 1993). From the trial transcript, we learn that Jennifer, the oldest of four children, began therapy in the fall of 1984 with an unlicensed New York psychotherapist for problems with her boyfriend and divided loyalties surrounding her parents' divorce. Over the next year or so she experienced recurring nightmares with violent themes, and waking terrors. Her therapist practiced a "Gestalt" method of therapy; Jennifer describes one session: "I started the same thing of shutting my eyes and just trying to feel the feelings and not let them go away really fast. And [my therapist] just said, 'Can you see anything?' . . . I couldn't see anything . . . and then all of a sudden I saw this carved bedpost from my room when I was a child. . . . And then I saw my father, and I could feel him sitting on the bed next to me, and he was pushing me down, and I was saying, 'No.' And he started pushing up my nightgown and . . . was touching me with his hands on my breast, and then between my legs, and then he was touching me with his mouth . . . and then it just all like went away. It was like . . . on TV if there is all static. . . . It was, all of a sudden it was plusssssh, all stopped. And then I slowly opened my eyes in the session and I said, 'I never knew that happened to me'" (pp. 58–59).

In one letter, written on January 11, 1989, to another rape survivor, [Jennifer H.] said that her father had raped her approximately 3,000 times.

Later Jennifer would have flashbacks that were so vivid that she could feel the lumpy blankets in her childhood bed. She remembered her father choking her and raping her in her parents' bedroom when she was about 12 or 13 (p. 91). She remembered her father threatening to rape her with a fishing pole in the den when she was about 6 or 7. She remembers her father raping her in the basement when she was in high school. The rape stopped just as her mother called down for them to come to dinner. She remembered her father raping her at her grandparents' home when she was in high school, while the large family was cooking and kids were playing. She remembered her father threatening to cut her with a letter opener, holding a kitchen knife to her throat (p. 113). She remembered him chasing her through the house with knives, trying to kill her, when she was about 13 years old (p. 283).

Jennifer also remembered a couple of incidents involving her mother. She remembered one time when she was raped in the bathroom and went to her mother wrapped in a towel with blood dripping. She remembered another incident, in which her father was raping her in her parents' bedroom and her mother came to the door and said, "David." The father then stopped raping her and went out to talk to the mother. Jennifer's mother said she had no recollection of these events, or of any sexual abuse. An expert witness testifying for Jennifer said it is common in cases of incest that mothers ignore the signs of abuse.

During the course of her memory development, Jennifer joined numerous sexual-abuse survivor groups. She read books about sexual abuse. She wrote columns. She contacted legislators. Jennifer was involved in years of therapy. She wrote letters about her abuse. In one letter, written to the President of Barnard College on February 7, 1987, she said, "I am a victim of incestuous abuse by my father and physical abuse by my mother" (p. 175). In another letter to her friend Jane, written in January 1988, she talked about her therapy: "Well, my memories came out . . . when I would sit and focus on my feelings which I believe I call visualization exercises because I would try to visualize what I was feeling or be able to bring into my eyes what I could see" (pp. 247–248). She told Jane about her Gestalt therapy: "In Gestalt therapy, the sub-personalities are allowed to take over and converse with one another and hopefully resolve their conflicts. Each personality gets a different chair, and when one new one starts to speak, the individual changes into that personality's seat. It sounds weird, and it is. But it is also an amazing journey into one's self. I've come to recognize untold universes within myself. It feels often very much like a cosmic battle when they are all warring with one another" (pp. 287–288; see also page 249).

In one letter, written on January 11, 1989, to another rape survivor, she said that her father had raped her approximately 3,000 times. In another letter, dated January 30, 1989, she wrote: "Underneath all the tinsel and glitter was my father raping me every two days. My mother smiling and pretending not to know what the hell was going on, and probably Dad abusing my siblings as well" (pp. 244-245). In a letter written on April 24, 1989, to *Mother Jones* magazine she said that she had survived hundreds of rapes by her father (p. 231).

Before October 1985, Jennifer testified, she didn't "know" that her father had ever put his penis in her vagina, or that he had put his penis in her mouth, or that he put his mouth on her vagina (p. 290). She paid her therapist $19,329.59 (p. 155) to acquire that knowledge.

In sum, Jennifer reported that she had been molested by her father from the ages of 4 to 17 (p. 239); that she was molested hundreds if not thousands of times, even if she could not remember all of the incidents; that this sometimes happened with many family members nearby, and with her mother's "involvement" in some instances; and that she buried these memories until she was 24, at which time they purportedly began to return to her. No one saw.

These are a few of the facts that the Kandels left out of their article. Jennifer was on the stand for nearly three days. She had "experts" to say they believed her memories were real. These experts were apparently unaware of, or unwilling to heed, Yapko's (1994) warnings about the impossibility, without independent corroboration, of distinguishing reality from invention and his urgings that symptoms by themselves cannot establish the existence of past abuse. At trial, Jennifer's father testified for about a half-hour (Kessler 1993b). How long does it take to say, "I didn't do it"? Oddly, his attorneys put on no character witnesses or expert testimony of their own, apparently believing—wrongly—that the implausibility of the "memories" would be enough. A Massachusetts jury awarded Jennifer $500,000.

Good and bad advice

Many of us would have serious reservations about the kinds of therapy activities engaged in by Jennifer H. and the kind of therapy practiced by the

Southwestern therapist who treated pseudopatient Ruth. Even recovered-memory supporters like Briere (1992) might agree. He did, after all, say quite clearly: "Unfortunately, a number of clients and therapists appear driven to expose and confront every possible traumatic memory" (p. 136). Briere notes that extended and intense effort to make a client uncover all traumatic material is not a good idea since this is often to the detriment of other therapeutic tasks, such as support, consolidation, desensitization, and emotional insight.

It is time to recognize that the dangers of false-memory creation are endemic to psychotherapy.

Some will argue that the vigorous exploration of buried sex-abuse memories is acceptable because it has been going on for a long time. In fact, to think it is fine to do things the way they've always been done is to have a mind that is as closed and dangerous as a malfunctioning parachute. It is time to recognize that the dangers of false-memory creation are endemic to psychotherapy (Lynn and Nash 1994). Campbell (1994) makes reference to Thomas Kuhn as he argues that the existing paradigm (the theories, methods, procedures) of psychotherapy may no longer be viable. When this happens in other professions, a crisis prevails and the profession must undertake a paradigm shift.

It may be time for that paradigm shift and for an exploration of new techniques. At the very least, therapists should not let sexual trauma overshadow all other important events in a patient's life (Campbell 1994). Perhaps there are other explanations for the patient's current symptoms and problems. Good therapists remain open to alternative hypotheses. Andreasen (1988), for example, urges practitioners to be open to the hypothesis of metabolic or neurochemical abnormalities as cause of a wide range of mental disorders. Even pharmacologically sophisticated psychiatrists sometimes refer their patients to neurologists, endocrinologists, and urologists. For less serious mental problems we may find, as physicians did before the advent of powerful antibiotics, that they are like many infections—self-limiting, running their course and then ending on their own (Adler 1994).

When it comes to serious diseases, a question that many people ask of their physicians is "How long have I got?" As Buckman and Sabbagh (1993) have aptly pointed out, this is a difficult question to answer. Patients who get a "statistical" answer often feel angry and frustrated. Yet an uncertain answer is often the truthful answer. When a psychotherapy patient asks, "Why am I depressed?" the therapist who refrains from giving an erroneous answer, however frustrating silence might be, is probably operating closer to the patient's best interests. Likewise, nonconventional "healers" who, relative to conventional physicians, give their patients unwarranted certainty and excess attention may make the patients temporarily feel better, but in the end may not be helping them at all.

Bad therapy based on bad theory is like a too-heavy oil that, instead of lubricating, can gum up the works—slowing everything down and heating everything up. When the mental works are slowed down and heated up, stray particles of false memory can, unfortunately, get stuck in it.

To avoid mucking up the works, constructive advice has been offered by Byrd (1994) and by Gold, Hughes, and Hohnecker (1994): Focus on enhancement of functioning rather than uncovering buried memories. If it is necessary to recover memories, do not contaminate the process with suggestions. Guard against personal biases. Be cautious about the use of hypnosis in the recovery of memories. Bibliotherapeutic and group therapy should not be encouraged until the patient has reasonable certainty that the sex abuse really happened. Development and evaluation of other behavioral and pharmacological therapies that minimize the possibility of false memories and false diagnoses should be encouraged.

Instead of dwelling on the misery of childhood and digging for childhood sexual trauma as its cause, why not spend some time doing something completely different. Borrowing from John Gottman's (1994) excellent advice on how to make your marriage succeed, patients might be reminded that negative events in their lives do not completely cancel out all the positives (p. 182). Encourage the patient to think about the positive aspects of life—even to look through picture albums from vacations and birthdays. Think of patients as the architects of their thoughts, and guide them to build a few happy rooms. The glass that's half empty is also half full. Gottman recognized the need for some real basis for positive thoughts, but in many families, as in many marriages, the basis does exist. Campbell (1994) offers similar advice. Therapists, he believes, should encourage their clients to recall some positive things about their families. A competent therapist will help others support and assist the client, and help the client direct feelings of gratitude toward those significant others.

Child abuse and accusations

We live in a culture of accusation. When it comes to molestation, the accused is almost always considered guilty as charged. Some claims of sexual abuse are as believable as any other reports based on memory, but others may not be. However, not all claims are true. As Reich (1994) has argued: "When we uncritically embrace reports of recovered memories of sexual abuse, and when we nonchalantly assume that they must be as good as our ordinary memories, we debase the coinage of memory altogether" (p. 38). Uncritical acceptance of every single claim of a recovered memory of sexual abuse, no matter how bizarre, is not good for anyone— not the client, not the family, not the mental-health profession, not the precious human faculty of memory. And let us not forget one final tragic consequence of overenthusiastic embracing of every supposedly derepressed memory; these activities are sure to trivialize the genuine memories of abuse and increase the suffering of real victims who wish and deserve, more than anything else, just to be believed.

We need to find ways of educating people who presume to know the truth. We particularly need to reach those individuals who, for some reason, feel better after they have led their clients—probably unwittingly— to falsely believe that family members have committed some terrible evil. If "truth" is our goal, then the search for evil must go beyond "feeling good" to include standards of fairness, burdens of proof, and presumptions of innocence. When we loosen our hold on these ideals, we risk a return to those times when good and moral human beings convinced themselves that a belief in the Devil meant proof of his existence. Instead, we should be marshaling all the science we can find to stop the modern-day Reverend Hale (from *The Crucible*), who if he lived today would still be telling anyone who would listen that he had seen "frightful proofs" that the Devil was alive. He would still be urging that we follow wherever "the accusing finger points"!

Note

1. John Mack details the kidnappings of 13 individuals by aliens, some of whom were experimented upon sexually. Mack believes their stories, and has impressed some journalists with his sincerity and depth of concern for the abductors (Neimark 1994). Carl Sagan's (1993:7) comment on UFO memories: "There is genuine scientific paydirt in UFO's and alien abductions—but it is, I think, of distinctly terrestrial origin."

References

Adler, J. 1994. The age before miracles. *Newsweek*, March 28, p. 44.

Andreasen, N.C. 1988. Brain imaging: Applications in psychiatry. *Science,* 239: 1381–1388.

Baker, R.A. 1992. *Hidden Memories.* Buffalo, N.Y.: Prometheus Books.

Briere, John N. 1992. *Child Abuse Trauma.* Newbury Park, Calif.: Sage Publications.

Buckman, R., and K. Sabbagh, 1993. *Magic or Medicine? An Investigation into Healing.* London: Macmillan.

Byrd, K.R. 1994. The narrative reconstructions of incest survivors. *American Psychologist,* 49:439–440.

Campbell, T.W. 1994. *Beware the Talking Cure.* Boca Raton, Fla.: Social Issues Resources Service (SirS).

Chu, J.A. 1992. The critical issues task force report: The role of hypnosis and amytal interviews in the recovery of traumatic memories. *International Society for the Study of Multiple Personality and Dissociation News,* June, pp. 6–9.

CNN. 1993. "Guilt by Memory." Broadcast on May 3.

Cronin, J. 1994. False memory. *Z Magazine.* April, pp. 31-37.

Gardner, R.A. 1991. *Sex Abuse Hysteria.* Creskill, N.J.: Creative Therapeutics.

Gold, Hughes, and Hohnecker. 1994. Degrees of repression of sexual-abuse memories. *American Psychologist,* 49:441–442.

Goldstein, E., and K. Farmer, eds. 1994. *True Stories of False Memories.* Boca Raton, Fla.: Social Issues Resources Service (SirS).

Gottman, J. 1994. *Why Marriages Succeed or Fail.* New York: Simon & Schuster.

Harris, M. 1974. *Cows, Pigs, Wars, and Witches: The Riddles of Culture.* New York: Vintage Books.

Hoult v. *Hoult.* 1993. Trial testimony. U.S. District Court for District of Massachusetts. Civil Action No 88-1738.

Kandel, M., and E. Kandel. 1994. Flights of memory. *Discover,* 15 (May): 32–37.

Kessler, G. 1993a. Memories of abuse. *Newsday,* November 28, pp. 1, 5, 54–55.

———. 1993b. Personal communication, *Newsday,* letter to EL dated December 13, 1993.

Lindsay, D.S., and J.D. Read. 1994. Psychotherapy and memories of childhood sexual abuse: A cognitive perspective. *Applied Cognitive Psychology,* 8:281–338.

Loftus, E.F. 1993. The reality of repressed memories. *American Psychologist,* 48:518–537.

Loftus, E.F., and K. Ketcham. 1994. *The Myth of Repressed Memory.* New York: St. Martin's Press.

Lynn, S.J., and M.R. Nash. 1994. Truth in memory. *American Journal of Clinical Hypnosis,* 36: 194–208.

Mack, J. 1994. *Abduction.* New York: Scribner's.

McHugh, P.R. 1992. Psychiatric misadventures. *American Scholar,* 61:497–510.

Neimark, J. 1994. The Harvard professor and the UFO's. *Psychology Today,* March-April, pp. 44–48, 74–90.

Poole, D., and D.S. Lindsay. 1994. "Psychotherapy and the Recovery of Memories of Childhood Sexual Abuse." Unpublished manuscript, Central Michigan University.

Rabinowitz, Dorothy. 1993. Deception: In the movies, on the news. *Wall Street Journal,* February 22. Review of television show "Not in My Family."

Reich, W. 1994. The monster in the mists. *New York Times Book Review,* May 15, pp. 1, 33–38.

Rogers, M.L. 1992. "A Case of Alleged Satanic Ritualistic Abuse." Paper presented at the American Psychology-Law Society meeting, San Diego, March.

Sagan, C. 1993. What's really going on? *Parade Magazine,* March 7, pp. 4–7.

Steele, D.R. 1994. Partial recall. *Liberty,* March, pp. 37–47.

Stevenson, I. 1994. A case of the psychotherapist's fallacy: Hypnotic regression to "previous lives." *American Journal of Clinical Hypnosis,* 36:188–193.

Trevor-Roper, H.R. 1967. *Religion, the Reformation, and Social Change.* London: Macmillan.

Trott, J. 1991. Satanic panic. *Cornerstone,* 20: 9–12.

Victor, J.S. 1991. Satanic cult "survivor" stories. *Skeptical Inquirer,* 15: 274–280.

Watson, B. 1992. Salem's dark hour: Did the devil make them do it? *Smithsonian,* 23: 117–131.

Yapko, M. 1994. *Suggestions of Abuse.* New York: Simon & Schuster.

6

Child Molestation Committed by Other Children Is a Serious Problem

Craig Horowitz

Craig Horowitz is a freelance writer and a contributing editor of New York *magazine.*

Studies show that a third of all cases of child sexual abuse are committed by other children and that many violent adult pedophiles began their activities as adolescents. The problem of children who molest is a serious one, but adolescent child molesters can be successfully treated through counseling and therapy programs. One such program offers adolescent sex offenders, who often have been abused themselves, the discipline and caring that their lives previously lacked.

Author's note: The names and some identifying details of all minors have been changed to protect privacy.

It had been a long time since Keith thought about getting caught, let alone came close to having it happen. But on this bright and balmy spring afternoon, he knew that if he didn't get his long legs pumping as high and as hard as he could, he'd be found out. Still, he stayed right where he was, behind a Dumpster in a deserted high school playground with his body pressed firmly on top of a 5-year-old girl.

She was his fourth victim. Over the last three years, Keith had sexually molested a 5-year-old and his two nieces, ages 6 and 7. He had become so confident he wouldn't be discovered that he'd been abusing the 6-year-old nearly every day for more than a year. But this day in the schoolyard was the first time he ventured away from his house to choose a victim at random. He spotted the little girl when she'd been left outside to play while her older brother went to a basketball game inside the school.

Now, however, the brother came looking for her. Every time she heard him call her name, she struggled fiercely to get up. And each time,

From Craig Horowitz, "Kids Who Prey on Kids," *Good Housekeeping*, October 1996. Reprinted by permission.

51

Keith pushed her down, hard. He held his hand over her face, and when she tried to scream anyway, he stuck his tongue in her mouth. But her brother's voice was getting louder as he got closer to the dumpster. Keith's heart raced, his breathing was heavy, and he could hear his own blood pounding in his ears. It wasn't fear; it was excitement. Even as time was running out on him, he continued to fondle the terrified little girl.

Finally she managed to let out a scream, and her brother came running. "He grabbed me by the neck and started beating me," Keith said later. "Every time he'd hit me I'd laugh. It didn't hurt—I actually didn't feel anything. He was getting angrier and hitting me harder. But I kept on laughing. I was provoking him because . . . I wanted him to kill me."

When the police came, Keith was charged with attempted sodomy and taken into custody. But he was back home that evening; a quick deal had been struck with prosecutors. That night he cut himself with a butcher knife, but his father was able to wrestle the knife away from him before he did any further damage. At 7:00 A.M. the next day, the police returned and drove him, not to jail, but to a treatment facility. Rather than punishment, he was offered therapy, a chance to turn his life around.

Why? Keith was 12 years old at the time of his arrest.

His first placement at a treatment center, which did not specialize in sex offenders, lasted only five months. So he was moved to the Pines Treatment Center in Portsmouth, VA, an intensive, highly structured program for juvenile sex offenders. He was placed on suicide watch; his room had no furniture, no windows, and a bed that was bolted to the floor. But after about a year and a half, Keith, a tall, redheaded teenager in a faded denim jacket, jeans, and a T-shirt, appeared to be making progress. The fact that he could admit what he'd done and take responsibility for the pain and suffering he had caused was an important and difficult step. He was no longer suicidal and, he said, his fantasies about rape and domination had stopped.

The Pines, started ten years ago, is one of the most respected programs of its kind in the country. Run by John Hunter, Ph.D., a clinical psychologist with nearly 20 years experience treating adolescent sex offenders, it is a small pocket of hope and enlightenment in what remains the least understood, least discussed, and perhaps most distressing area of child sex abuse: kids who prey on other kids.

The problem of children who molest

The national debate over how to deal with adult sex offenders continues to rage: Should they be punished, or treated? Should they be locked up permanently, or paroled? And even after New Jersey passed Megan's Law, requiring police to notify community members when released offenders move into their town, the controversy over the usefulness and constitutionality of this approach remains heated. Confronting the problem of children who are child molesters is even more confounding. And making the issue more pressing are new findings that show that more than 50 percent of the adults arrested for sex crimes began their aberrant behavior as juveniles.

Like Keith, most of the 112 children currently at the Pines were placed there by the courts as an alternative to (depending on their ages) a juvenile detention center or prison. Also, like Keith, many of them have suffered physical and sexual abuse themselves. Keith's mother beat and sexually molested him; so did her boyfriend. When he was 2½, his mother locked him in the bathroom with her while she slit her wrists and bled all over him. When Keith was taken away from her by authorities that same year, he was bounced to a dozen different foster homes in two years before he was taken in, at 5, by a family who adopted him.

If Keith's case were isolated, experts wouldn't think a crisis is upon us. But more and more instances of kids committing sexually deviant acts are coming to light. Around the country, police, prosecutors, and social-service workers are struggling to deal with the rise in the number of juvenile sex offenders. Much of the increase is due to the higher visibility of the problem and, therefore, better reporting of abuse, but experts won't rule out a bona fide increase. "In the past, people frequently wrote off everything as 'sexually exploratory behavior.' But I can say, anecdotally, that there's much more physical aggression and violence shown by today's children," says Judith Becker, Ph.D., a professor of psychology and psychiatry at the University of Arizona. "I've gotten referrals for seven- and eight-year-olds who have serious sexual behavior problems."

New findings . . . show that more than 50 percent of the adults arrested for sex crimes began their aberrant behavior as juveniles.

According to researchers' most conservative approximations, juveniles now commit one third of all the sexual abuse reported every year. Beyond that, reliable numbers are impossible to come by. It's only recently that the FBI has even recognized the need to compile statistics about adolescent sex crimes. Further clouding the picture is the varied definition of what constitutes abuse between juveniles. In some states, for example, there must be a minimum age difference of, say, four years, between the predator and the victim before sexual contact is considered abuse. Other states recognize a sexual encounter as abusive only when the offender is not only older but is also someone in a position of trust, like a baby-sitter or counselor.

Although there aren't bankable statistics to define the breadth of the problem, there's certainly other evidence. When the Pines opened as an eight-bed facility in 1986, there were no more than two or three other centers like it in the country. Today, there are hundreds of similar programs— with enough troubled children to keep them all busy. At first, the overwhelming majority of victimizers referred to the Pines were boys between the ages of 15 and 18. Now the Pines regularly treats both boys and girls of all races and socio-economic backgrounds, from as young as age 10.

Though the known number of young girls who become sexual predators is still relatively small, it is growing. Hunter says that girls are now responsible for 5 percent of the reported abuse of other girls and 20 percent of the cases involving boys. Although half of all the boys Hunter sees are physically abused, and between half and three quarters are sexually abused, for girls the percentages for both climb to between 75 and 90 percent.

But if the abuse these children have suffered is so brutal, if the pain runs so deep, and if the impact on their personalities is so profound, can they be helped? Can years of almost unspeakable horrors be overcome by a year-or-two stay at a treatment center, no matter how good the program is? Yes, say experts, who argue that kids are remarkably resilient, and that all but a small percentage of them can be turned around.

A program for juvenile child molesters

Housed on a sprawling 30-acre campus, the Pines, with its dormitories, tennis courts, basketball hoops, gym, and pool, looks like a small college. But this is not a place of leisure. The Pines provides a regimen of discipline and the teaching of values. Its guiding philosophy and its success are the result of the vision and the passion of Hunter.

"So many of these kids have never had a positive male role model," says Hunter, who has three sons of his own ranging in age from 12 to 25. "We teach them right from wrong. And when we're successful, an emotional bond develops. Two or three or four years after they leave the program they write just to say hello and to tell us how they're doing."

Each child in the program has an individual therapist (many with a Ph.D. or a master's degree) and is monitored 24 hours a day; no one is alone for more than 15 minutes at a time, and even during the night, someone patrols the hallways to make sure every child stays in his or her own room. Although such vigilant supervision might seem like a given at this kind of a facility, many of the kids tell stories about their stays at other treatment centers, where it was easy to have sex with other kids. At the Pines, such transgressions are hard to imagine, since there is one staff member for every three kids.

The Pines treats its residents for all the disorders that plague them—a significant distinction given that 30 to 40 percent of those in the Pines have learning disabilities and one third are clinically depressed. It also has its own fully accredited, on-site school (middle through high school), which not only serves the practical function of enabling kids to attend classes without having to leave the center, but also provides an opportunity to observe the kids outside of a clinical setting.

Crucial feedback comes from the counselors who are with the residents in the spare, dorm-style rooms where they relax, do homework, and sleep. The rooms, each equipped with a bed, desk, small closet, and bathroom, are single- or double-occupancy.

At the Pines, residents follow three phases of treatment, each running 16 weeks. Along with group therapy, family therapy when possible, and individual counseling sessions, each young offender attends daily community meetings. Before anyone can graduate to the next phase, they must prove, in Hunter's words, that "they're getting it." A careful assessment is made based on written and oral tests as well as staff observations. This kind of comprehensive program is costly, and the bill is about $275 a day per resident. It's paid for with state funds, ultimately from taxpayer money. A tiny portion of residents pay privately.

Phase one, in which boys and girls are segregated, focuses on getting the kids to recognize what they've done, comprehend society's laws and values, and learn impulse control and coping techniques.

But first Hunter must get their attention. One of the most effective ways to do this is to remind them that "treatment is a privilege and not a right. I believe very strongly in making sure the older kids get charged in court. It's a heck of a motivator when we can tell them that if they blow it now, they're going to jail."

Getting juveniles' attention

One recent afternoon, Hunter addressed a group of new residents. He stood at the front of a wood-paneled room, facing a familiar scene: eight angry, laconic teens sitting with their arms folded across their chests, some with their unlaced-sneakered feet slung over the backs of the furniture in front of them. A couple slumped in their chairs, as if they were trying to slither away and disappear. And there was one boy in particular whom Hunter kept his eye on: Rick, 16, who was here for sexually molesting his 11-year-old sister, had also been caught shoplifting and setting fires. He'd been at the Pines only a week but he'd already had so many scuffles with the staff that he was on the verge of being kicked out.

As Hunter pushed, chastised, challenged, and threatened, several of the boys seemed to tune him out. Rick sat, sullen but quiet, as Hunter began playing a videotape.

Almost immediately something in the room changed. The boys straightened up and focused on the screen. What riveted them was a five-year-old death-row interview with convicted pedophile and child killer Westley Alan Dodd, conducted shortly before he was executed. Dodd talked about the fact that he became a sexual predator as an adolescent and that the criminal justice system simply didn't take him seriously. Though he confessed nine times to police, he was prosecuted only three times, and never served more than four months in prison. He wasn't required to get treatment. "All I'm trying to do is convince people that something needs to be done. You've got to work with the juvenile offenders." As time went on, Dodd told the interviewer, he was neither punished nor treated, and his deviant acts became progressively more serious. "Finally, killing was the only thing left."

According to researchers' most conservative approximations, juveniles now commit one third of all the sexual abuse reported every year.

Though Dodd was only 29 at the time of the interview, he was ready to die. He looked straight into the camera and said he knew it was too late for him. If he were released from prison, he said dispassionately, he would kill again. "Is there anybody who cares about you?" the interviewer asked him. "No." "Do you care about yourself?" "No."

"This tape always gets the kids' attention," says Hunter. But on this particular afternoon the response was especially strong. Even Rick seemed transformed. "He came up to me afterward," says Hunter, "and said, 'I couldn't believe it, but I saw myself on that tape. I could easily be that person. I can see where I'm headed.' He proceeded to sit down and talk about treatment. He's still in the program and doing reasonably well now."

When the kids reach the final stage of the program, they learn what is perhaps the most important thing they will take with them from the Pines: empathy. Many enter the Pines after years of struggling to protect themselves. They survive by disconnecting and insulating themselves: Like Dodd, they believe, "Nobody cares about me, so why should I care about anyone else?" Often the only role models they've had have been either extremely aggressive or extremely helpless.

"For these kids, the threat of getting caught is not enough to stop them," says Hunter. "They must get in touch with their inner hurt or they'll never understand how their aggression hurts their victims." A critical element of this process, when it's successful, is the completion of a letter that the offenders write to their victims and their victims' families. In it, they must accept responsibility for what they've done, apologize, and explain that they now understand the terrible impact they've had. The letters are an exercise; they're never actually mailed, since experts agree that most victims do not welcome being drawn in to molesters' rehabilitation attempts.

Returning juvenile molesters to their homes

Keith graduated from the Pines in September 1995, after almost a two-year stay. Before he went home, he did a short stint at a group home, a pause intended to give his family time to adjust to his return. He's now back in high school, where he takes special-ed classes because of a learning disability diagnosed at the Pines. He keeps his appointments with a therapist and a probation officer and has not committed any new sex crimes. But he is clearly not completely healed; since his release, he's gotten in trouble for truancy, minor drug possession, and fire-setting, none of which has resulted in an arrest.

Still, the families of many graduates talk about a level of success and progress. "I'm really thankful I had somewhere to turn. In the beginning, I had no idea this was going on in my house," says one mother from Portsmouth, whose two sons, 14 and 16, had been abusing their 11-year-old sister since she was 7. The situation came to light only when the little girl saw a film about child abuse at school and told a teacher that that was being done to her. The mother eventually found out that her ex-husband, who years earlier had kidnaped her children, had sexually abused them during the five and a half years they lived with him.

The boys have graduated from the Pines and now are living with relatives. Their sister is in therapy and is not ready for them to come home yet. "The family is an integral part of the treatment," says Hunter. "We work whenever possible toward family reunification. Kids need to know that there's someone out there who cares about them."

Hunter is hopeful when he looks at the progress that's been made during the last 15 years. "I got into this work because I saw mental-health practitioners treating victimizers with traditional therapies that just didn't seem to be effective," he says. "I believed this was a problem that deserved scientific inquiry. The majority of the kids do respond, and without this help they would surely continue to offend."

7
Child Molestation Committed by Other Children Is Not a Widespread Problem

Judith Levine

Judith Levine is the author of the forthcoming book In Search of Innocence: America's Battle over Children's Sexuality.

A group of influential psychotherapists has created a moral panic by exaggerating the problem of "children who molest." Yet these therapists have produced no research indicating how so-called child sex offenders differ in sexual behavior from normal adolescents. Overzealous child protection workers, encouraged by the child welfare system to report any suspicion of child sexual abuse, created a nightmare for one family when they accused a nine-year-old boy of being a budding sex offender.

Author's note: The names and identifying characteristics of the family members have been changed.

Tony Diamond is a troubled boy. Charming and tractable one minute, he may be flailing in rage or brooding in despair the next. Tony's classwork is outstanding; he reads widely and writes winningly. In a report on Napoleon, he quotes the "battleous" (and apparently bilingual) "military genius" as uttering the famous palindrome, "Able was I ere I saw Elba." Yet he fights and disobeys at school—and in his short life he's attended several.

Portrait of a juvenile sex offender?

Like other boys his age, 12, Tony likes *Star Wars* and baseball. He takes care of a small menagerie at home—a hamster, a rabbit, and a garrulous

From Judith Levine, "A Question of Abuse," *Mother Jones*, July/August 1996. Reprinted with permission from *Mother Jones* magazine, ©1996, Foundation for National Progress.

cockatiel. But he can be mean to his sister, Jessica, one year his junior, dark and soft where he is blond and slender, slow in class where he excels. Their relationship, it seems, is fierce—fiercely affectionate and fiercely antagonistic. One evening, they sit next to each other, playing quietly. Another time, she climbs into the car and he slaps her.

Three years ago, in November 1993, San Diego County Child Protective Services pronounced Tony a grave danger to his sister. Jessie had told someone at school that her brother had "touched her private parts, front and back." Mandated by the 1974 Child Abuse Prevention and Treatment Act to report any suspicion of child abuse, even by a child and even without substantiation, Jessica's elementary school called the Child Abuse Hotline. A social worker elicited a record of Tony's earlier offenses: In elementary school, he used sexual language and looked under girls' skirts; at 4, he lay on top of Jessie in the bath.

Now, sex abuse hysteria has delivered a new kind of perpetrator: "children who molest."

San Diego Juvenile Court charged Tony with "sexual abuse" of Jessica "including, but not limited to, touching her vaginal and anal areas . . . placing a pencil in her buttocks," and threatening to hurt her if she "disclosed the molest."

"It would appear from a review of the case," the social worker wrote, "that Tony is a budding sex offender." Tony was 9 years old.

What followed for the Diamonds was a nightmare, executed by a system so zealous to protect children from perceived sexual abuse that it may fracture their families and crush their spirits in the process. First Tony and then Jessica were removed from their mother's home and placed in state custody. Only after more than two years of foster and group homes, treatment programs, and the representation of a private lawyer, would the family be reunited.

But blame for the Diamond family's travails cannot be assigned exclusively to San Diego County caseworkers, therapists, and judges. They, like many of the nation's journalists, politicians, and parents, suspect sex abusers are everywhere and include everyone—the competent teacher, the friendly neighbor, the loving father. Now, sex abuse hysteria has delivered a new kind of perpetrator: "children who molest."

These kids, as young as 2, are diagnosed and treated, and sometimes prosecuted, for "inappropriate" behaviors like diddling, licking, putting things inside genitals, flashing, mooning, or masturbating "compulsively." They are accused of "coercion," though often the sex play is consensual.

Some kids have committed real sexual intrusions on other kids. But while these children are almost always aggressive in other ways—they fight, steal, or set fires, for example—the unproved assumption, deeply embedded in American psychological ideology, is that sex is a wholly different, and worse, category of behavior, profoundly symptomatic for the doer and inevitably traumatic for the done-to.

So, with little supportive evidence, the new children-who-molest experts have persuaded the child protective systems they work for that "sex-offense-specific" therapy is necessary for any kid with a "sexual behavior problem." They insist this therapy, whose methodologies derive from their own theories, can be practiced only by them or others they have trained.

When Diane Diamond invited a caseworker into her blue-and-beige adobe house, she had a naive faith in the helping professions. The quick, blond woman had undergone plenty of healing herself, by both traditional and new age practitioners, and in several Child Protective Services interviews she poured out her family's history in sentences studded with psychologisms.

She told the caseworkers that, pregnant with Jessica, she'd fled the children's father, who had beaten and raped her and had choked 1-year-old Tony; she reported that a man had exposed himself to Jessica in the park, and she'd tried to press charges; she said that the children might have been encouraged in sexual play by a babysitter years earlier. Diane told Child Protective Services she was concerned about her son's volatility and depression; she thought he might even be suicidal, and she hoped they'd help find him therapy.

Twenty years ago that might have happened. The school could have referred Diane to a child or family therapist to deal with the whole constellation of her children's needs. But today, teachers and social workers, undereducated in psychology and overtrained (often by law enforcers) in sexual abuse, tend to see sexual pathology and criminal exploitation in any situation that looks even remotely sexual.

So Diane's tale turned against her, becoming a sort of stationhouse confession about a criminally insane family: Tony had a history of abuse (a psychologist wrote that he had "witnessed" his mother's rape, though he was only months old); the possible abuse by a babysitter was recorded as though it were a certain and traumatic event; Jessica's glimpse of the flasher's penis was added to her list of victimizations. Because Diane was at the time more worried about Tony than about Jessica, who seemed OK, Child Protective Services decided Diane was "minimizing" the "molestation," and judged her incapable of protecting her daughter.

Tony was declared a "sex offender," made a ward of the San Diego dependency court, and removed from his mother's custody.

Sexual abuse panics in San Diego

Panic over child abuse seems to sprout from the desert soil of San Diego as abundantly as neon fuchsia succulents and bougainvillea. The county has been the scene of a string of highly publicized false allegations of molestation, including satanic ritual abuse, going back to the 1980s. In 1992, a major grand jury investigation found the county's child welfare agencies and juvenile courts to be "a system out of control," so keen on protecting children from predation that it took hundreds of them away from their parents on what turned out to be false charges. The report called for "profound change" throughout the system.

Carol Hopkins, deputy forewoman of that grand jury, now chairs the Justice Committee, which works to overturn false convictions of satanic ritual abuse and child abuse. She says some of the changes were instituted, but that many of the same people are still working in the child protection system. When cases of kids accused of abuse started crossing her desk, with these same names on them, Hopkins felt queasy. "This," she thought, "is the next satanic ritual abuse."

San Diego Union-Tribune reporter Mark Sauer saw it coming, too. In the early 1990s, he watched psychologist Toni Cavanagh Johnson and social worker Kee MacFarlane presenting their work on children who molest at a professional conference held in San Diego. He was astonished. "First they state that there is no research—that we really don't know anything about normal children's sexual behavior," he recalls. "Then out come the pie charts and graphs and they go on for an hour defining this new abnormality. And everybody is madly taking notes."

Sauer had reason to be suspicious of MacFarlane and the clinic she worked for, Children's Institute International in Los Angeles. His newspaper had published some of the only skeptical coverage of the 1980s McMartin Preschool satanic ritual abuse trials. Sauer knew MacFarlane as the woman who headed the team that interrogated nearly 400 children for the prosecution and found 369 to have been victimized in bizarre rituals including anal rape, animal mutilation, and kidnapping through secret tunnels. Except for one, none of the children mentioned abuse until they got to CII. After the jury saw MacFarlane's taped interviews, full of leading, hectoring questions, they voted to acquit the defendants.

Johnson, now the children-who-molest guru, had not yet joined CII at the time of the McMartin interviews, but became affiliated with the clinic and began working with MacFarlane in 1985. She left the clinic in 1990, and her tenure is not mentioned in her publicity materials. It was Johnson who first coined the diagnostic description, "children who molest," in a 1988 paper, while working with MacFarlane at CII's Support Program for Abusive Reactive Kids. Since then, her 1993 book, *Sexualized Children: Assessment and Treatment of Sexualized Children and Children Who Molest*, co-authored with psychologist Eliana Gil, has become the specialty's main text.

How big is this problem?

As in the satanic ritual abuse scare, the prophets of this plague claim the problem is enormous, but we don't see it because we aren't looking hard enough. "[Children who molest] make all of us uncomfortable," writes MacFarlane in her 1996 book, *When Children Abuse*, "so uncomfortable, we've had to deny their existence and/or minimize their behavior until now. We've called their behavior 'exploration' or 'curiosity' until they were old enough for us to comfortably call it what it is: sexual abuse of other children.

"Who are they?" she continues. "So far, relatively few have come to our attention."

In fact, arrests for juvenile sex offenses are up in many states. Although this demonstrates increasing alertness on the part of the juvenile justice system, it does not necessarily indicate that juvenile sex offenses are on the rise. Police records are unenlightening about what exactly is happening between children—the courts label as a "sexual offense" everything from consensual fondling between different-age kids to forced sodomy. It's even harder to tell what's happening in the dependency courts, where younger kids are sent, because those records are confidential.

Moreover, the 1974 Child Abuse Prevention and Treatment Act offered an incentive to rout out alleged sexual abuse: States get federal matching funds for programs that identify and treat abused kids and prosecute their abusers, including minor offenders. Since then, child abuse reports have grown dramatically. But of the 2.9 million child abuse reports filed in 1993, two-thirds could not be substantiated.

Despite a near-absolute absence of normative data about what kids actually do sexually, literature on this new category of juvenile "deviance" is filling up the child abuse bibliographies. In 1984, there were no treatment programs for such kids. Today, the Vermont-based Safer Society Foundation database lists 50 residential and 396 nonresidential programs that treat "sex offenders" under 12. And at the 1995 Association for the Treatment of Sex Abusers conference, about 80 percent of the exhibition tables featured literature on such programs for children and adolescents.

As the diagnosis of "sexual behavior problems" gains currency in sex abuse circles, it is also on its way to wider ratification, which in turn will boost media attention, funding, and business. Two five-year, $1 million studies that provided therapy and evaluated the best treatment approach for hundreds of "sexualized" children under 12 are just wrapping up in Vermont, Oklahoma, and Washington. And if this major grant from the government's National Center on Child Abuse and Neglect (NCCAN) does not institutionalize the new sickness, some psychologists are promoting the inclusion of juvenile sex offending into the *Diagnostic and Statistical Manual of Mental Disorders*, or *DSM*, the canon of psychopathologies.

For more than two years, almost a score of adults—foster parents, social workers, psychologists, and judges—evaluated, disciplined, and relocated Tony, planned his treatments (few of which he received), supervised his relationship with his family, and generated thousands of pages of paper.

Tony was found to be in need of "boundaries." So he was placed with a foster mother, who kept him inside much of the day, stored his toys on an inaccessible shelf in the garage, and punished him when he was "manipulative," by making him sit on the stairs for hours. Later, the foster mother accused Tony of "sexual assault" for pushing against her while she was doing dishes. (Tony's court-appointed therapist, Philip Kaushall, interviewed the boy about the incident. "I don't believe he did it," Kaushall reported.)

Of the 2.9 million child abuse reports filed in 1993, two-thirds could not be substantiated.

From the start, Child Protective Services identified Jessie as the victim, though it will probably never be known how much of the sex play between the siblings was consensual. In fact, Jessie later told a social worker that one of the main incidents that put her brother in foster care didn't even involve disrobing. Tony "poked her with a pencil over the clothes. The pencil wasn't inside her body. He just hurt her a little and she didn't like it," the social worker reported.

Jessie was getting attention for talking about abuse. In May 1994, she told a different social worker her mother had sexually abused her by lying on top of her in bed. (She also said a social worker "wanted to molest" her, but this charge was not investigated.) Later, at least one psychologist would find the girl unable to "differentiate between imagination and reality."

When Jessie's mother, whose criminal record consisted of one unpaid fine for a broken taillight, explained that she'd reached across her daughter to turn off the electric blanket, Child Protective Services found her "in denial." The agency made a "true finding" of abuse, and took Jessie from Diane and sent her to a foster home, too.

Normal sexual behavior among children

What potential harm could justify removing two small children from a mother whose only observed transgression was a distrust of the child protective authorities?

Barbara Bonner, who is running the largest component of the five-year NCCAN studies, in Oklahoma City, acknowledges that such interventions are "driven by values," because the science of child sexual development is so paltry.

"We will probably never know the harm [of children behaving sexually], because no one will ever do that with those kids—let them get inappropriately involved with other children [in a clinical setting]," she explains. "They might become oversexually stimulated and prefer sexual behavior to sports, dance, or other more appropriate activities. They might become promiscuous as adults. But we don't have long-term outcomes. They may turn out to be normal."

Nonetheless, she says, "We recommend, as people who are hopefully knowledgeable, and as a society, what we consider to be appropriate and in the best interest of children." Her program's "sexual behavior rules" for 6- to 11-year-olds include not touching others' "private parts" or letting others touch or see theirs.

Toni Johnson also says that some sexual behavior among kids is OK. "Normal, healthy sexuality is what we need in children. There is no problem with that," she said in an interview. "You think we are out looking to condemn children's sexual behaviors. For the last eight years, I have been talking on this continuum. You are finding the extraordinary cases." What defines molestation, says Johnson, is sex that is aggressive or nonconsensual.

The position sounds reasonable, except that Johnson and her followers define unhealthy "aggression" on their own terms, often dismissing the children's experience—most notably when the victim does not feel victimized. "I don't know if it's the degree of pleasantness or unpleasantness that ought to be the guideline that determines whether it is appropriate or not," says Bonner. "The victim should be defined by somebody other than the child."

But sexologist Leonore Tiefer suggests that even coercive aggression ought not necessarily be pathologized. "Kids push and hit and demand, until they're socialized," she said.

In fact, a study of 128 psychologically healthy Bryn Mawr College students, who wrote about their thrilling games of porn star, rapist, and slave girl when they were young, indicates that even "force may exist on a continuum" within normative child sex play. Definitions of consent are not cut and dried.

And therein lies the problem: Except in the most benign games of doctor between children of the same age, the children-who-molest experts generally rule out the possibility that any underage child can consent to sex.

In his "Pathways" workbook for youthful sexual transgressors, Bellevue, Wash., social worker Tim Kahn tells readers that to consent, "the partner must understand the proposed action, know what society's standards are for this action, [and] be aware of the consequences and alternatives." Then how can a child who is not a lawyer consent to sex? "Children don't know what they are consenting to," Kahn states. "They need to be protected from more manipulative or sophisticated persons."

The assumptions of children-who-molest theories

So why not improve sex education, rather than stigmatize sex by rushing kids to a specialist? The reasoning lies in two main elements of children-who-molest theory. The first—a corollary of the so-called cycle of abuse—is that "age-inappropriate" behavior is a symptom that the perpetrator is himself a victim of abuse. (Where else, the logic goes, would a 7-year-old get the idea of putting a crayon, or a penis, into somebody's vagina?) Although this is sometimes true, even Johnson admits that plenty of kids who have sex are not abused. Yet the term "abuse-reactive" is used almost universally when describing "sex abusers" under 12, and social workers and law enforcement professionals facing "inappropriate" sexual behavior by children almost automatically suspect the parents.

The second element is the belief that sex acts by children are often more coercive than we think and therefore must be stopped, lest the perpetrator grow up to become a bona fide molester.

"[Adult] offenders will tell you they started out young, maybe masturbating in public," says Bill Southwell, co-chair of a countywide task force on juvenile sex offenders. (Southwell also supervised the San Diego County sheriff's child abuse unit from 1985 to 1988 and from 1991 to 1994, when it conducted some infamously flawed investigations.)

However, the fact that adult offenders experimented sexually as children doesn't mean that children who experiment become sex offenders; prison and clinical populations simply don't represent the general population, says Temple University psychology professor Bruce Rind.

In any case, the children-who-molest theorists argue that even if a kid is not being abused, and even if he won't become a grown-up abuser, "age-inappropriate" sex is a sign of emotional distress. Johnson alerts parents to be concerned if a child exhibits at least three "problematic" behaviors, like wanting to be naked in public, using dirty words after being told "no," or "touch[ing] the genitals of animals," and to seek professional help if he asks "endless questions about sex."

What's wrong with these things? "They make parents nervous," says Allie Kilpatrick, a social work professor at the University of Georgia who conducted a massive review of the literature on childhood sexual experiences, both wanted and unwanted, and administered her own 33-page questionnaire to 501 Southern women. Most of Kilpatrick's subjects had kissed and hugged, fondled and masturbated as adolescents, and more than a quarter had had vaginal intercourse. Her conclusion: "The majority of young people who experience some kind of sexual behavior find it pleasurable, without much guilt, and with no harmful consequences." A similar study of 526 New England undergraduates revealed "no differences . . . between sibling, nonsibling, and no-[sexual]-experience groups on a variety of adult sexual behavior and sexual adjustment measures."

Around the globe, just about everything Johnson considers worrisome is unremarkable. Clellan Ford and Frank Beach, in the classic 1951 *Patterns of Sexual Behavior*, examined 191 of the world's peoples, including Americans. "As long as the adult members of a society permit them to do so," they noted, "immature males and females engage in practically every type of sexual behavior found in grown men and women."

In fact, most sexologists say that the trauma of kids' sex usually comes not from the sex itself, but from adults getting upset about it.

Despite Child Protective Services' official intentions, Tony got almost no therapy until November 1994, when Philip Kaushall, a psychologist the county had appointed to supervise family visits, agreed to conduct joint sessions with Tony's mother. When he met the Diamonds that summer, Kaushall was shocked that the children were in foster care: He recognized troubles in the family, but nothing that warranted separation. In September, he began recommending to the authorities that the kids go home.

Around that time, Jessica started attending Daughters and Sons United, an incest treatment group, where she reported learning about "good and bad guilt," the latter of which she understood as "when you tell on somebody about something and you feel bad about it." She'd come out of those meetings angry and excited, recalls Diane. "And she'd go, 'I'm gonna report you, Mother,' every time she got mad." Meanwhile, Jessie's therapist was repeatedly asking the girl about "bad things that might happen" if the children went home, according to a social worker's report.

The fact that adult offenders experimented sexually as children doesn't mean that children who experiment become sex offenders.

Both children's therapy continued, but what went on in Kaushall's office did not fulfill Tony's requirement to undergo "offender treatment" with a therapist specifically trained in children-who-molest theory. So, in October 1995, almost two years after the "offense," Juvenile Court put Tony in a "sexually reactive children's" group with social worker David McWhirter, among the county's most prominent therapists of juvenile offenders. (McWhirter also runs a treatment program for older children.)

But soon McWhirter, who describes the children's group work as "soft confrontation," wrote Kaushall to inform him that Tony was disruptive. The boy didn't want to confess guilt, the first step required for "recovery," and was doubtful of the other kids' guilt, too. ("Mom," he reported one afternoon, "there's one kid in there for mooning!")

Kaushall encouraged Tony and Diane to cooperate, but he says that privately he felt McWhirter's approach might be a failure from the get-go.

"There may be a need for therapy," says Kaushall. "But if you treat somebody specifically for a 'sex offense,' you are undercutting the treatment automatically, because you give them an identity as a sex offender, which is precisely what you don't want them to have."

The treatment catch-22

The treatment of sex offenders, including little ones, is classic good cop–bad cop stuff. The theory sounds like children's rights propaganda: promote self-esteem and empathy, consent and equality. But the practice is anything but fair, and the rights of both kids and parents are all but disregarded. A patient receives no due process: As long as he protests his innocence, he is "in denial" and he can be dropped from the program—without which he can't get out of state custody. Worse: His treatment, unlike a jail sentence, may go on indefinitely.

The American Civil Liberties Union Prison Project has sued a number of similar programs for adults, including one in Vermont, whose "drama therapy" portion compelled inmates to simulate anal rape while the therapist shouted obscenities at them. (The program's director, William Pithers, is now co-director of the Vermont component of the NCCAN study to devise treatment for sexualized children.)

Parents who take exception to either the charges or the treatment are considered part of the problem. Usually mandated to therapy themselves, they are counseled to overlook their own judgment, stop trusting their kids, and heed their betters.

And if parents do not bite the carrot of "cure," the stick isn't far away. "In cases where children are very young and families are not very cooperative, it may require a Dependency Court petition regarding neglect, failure to supervise, or other category addressing parental responsibility in order to compel parents to cooperate with recommended living arrangements and treatment plans," writes MacFarlane in *When Children Abuse*. In plain English: Resist treatment and risk losing your kid.

Diane Diamond's resistance to the state's approach to her family's problem became the main impediment to her getting her kids back. "You should be aware that your conduct at Tony's birthday party . . . was inappropriate and detrimental to your reunification efforts," wrote one caseworker, enumerating her transgressions. Among them: "You put your arms around Tony's neck and whispered into his ear."

Once the narrative was inscribed—crazy mother makes boy a molester, victimizes girl—no alternative story could be told. When Jessie confessed to a social worker, almost immediately, that she had "told lies" about her mother's alleged molesting, social workers presumed her to be exhibiting accommodation syndrome, that is, suffering the consequences of being removed from the life she knew and thus lying to put things back as they were.

Diane sold her car and hired a private lawyer to try to get her children back. She spent Christmas of 1994 alone, while the hearing was delayed. In February 1995, she had her day in dependency court—and lost. Tony was sent to yet another foster home, where he began losing weight and hope. Jessie was in her seventh foster home, pleading to be returned to her mother. Kaushall wrote report after report to Child Protective Services that institutionalization and separation from their mother was damaging the children, and that Diane's home was the best place for them.

As it happens, after 18 months of holding a child in custody, federal law requires that the dependency court come up with a permanent plan—to send him home, place him in long-term foster care, appoint a guardian, or terminate the parents' rights and refer him for adoption. Yet it took an additional seven months before Child Protective Services made arrangements to move Tony and Jessica back home. The final outcome of the Diamonds' case appears to be a combination of bureaucratic fatigue, Diane's refusal to give up her children without a savage fight, and Kaushall's intervention, which may have prevented the children from being put up for adoption.

The splintered family was reunited early this year [1996], although Jessie will officially remain in state custody until this fall.

Over the past two centuries, the arbiters of deviance have moved from the pulpit to the clinic. But, as Barbara Bonner suggests, "normal" remains a moral category. And, just as 19th-century doctors who surgically "cured" masturbation and Progressive Era judges who sent girls to reform school for sexual "precociousness" were enforcing the social-religious order, today's diagnosers of "childhood sexual behavior problems" reveal a terror of pleasurable excess and an anger at kids who won't buckle under sexual taboos.

The same moralistic intolerance of desire quashes the behavioral research critical to stemming real perils, like the spread of AIDS and teen pregnancy. Congress' reauthorization of the National Institutes of Health in 1993, for example, specifically prohibited appropriations for sexuality surveys, moving those moneys to programs that promote premarital celibacy.

"This all reminds me of heroic gynecology [during the early 20th century], which regarded the birth process itself as a pathological thing," says Vern Bullough, a distinguished professor emeritus at State University of New York (SUNY) who has written or edited over 50 books on sexuality. "What we've got now is heroic intervention in childhood sexuality by people who don't know what they are talking about."

What we've got now is heroic intervention in childhood sexuality by people who don't know what they are talking about.

Kaushall says he is equally disgusted. "There is no doubt in my mind that what was done [to the Diamonds] was 100 times worse than any problem they had to begin with. It was handled with a lethal combination of zealotry and incompetence."

Jessie, he believes, "has learned that when she talks about sex, everyone will drop their forks and knives and listen. She knows sex is a powerful weapon." The "sex offender" Tony suffered harshness and betrayal from adults; he is depressed and mistrustful. For both kids, Kaushall says, "the developmental harm of breaking a bond with the parent is tremendous."

On a bright Sunday in March [1996], though, everybody seems OK.

Jessie goes off to an "ugly dog show" with a church volunteer, and the rest of us drive to La Jolla to wade in the tide pools. Tony hugs his mom frequently, demands to go to McDonald's, and mopes when he doesn't get to. "I'm a survivor," Diane tells me, estimating that her ordeal has cost more than $30,000. She chats about "our plans" to move to Arizona—or maybe Oregon, she says, because "we love the beach." She uses "we" often, as if to repossess that fragile pronoun.

Tony and I peel snails from a rock as Diane explains that I am writing about their family. His brown eyes become serious, and he asks: "Are you writing about cruelty to children in California?"

8

Priest Child Molesters Disgrace the Catholic Priesthood

John J. Dreese

John J. Dreese is a Catholic priest in Columbus, Ohio.

The scandal of priest pedophilia has hurt not only the victims of child sexual abuse but the church and priesthood as well. The church should have confronted this problem long ago. Formerly, priests who committed sexual offenses were treated either as sinners or as mentally ill. They were given penance or counseling and then moved to another parish. This was a bad policy; however, treating these priests as criminals now may not help them or their victims to recover.

The constant reporting by the media of the sexual abuse of children and adolescents by priests has become a kind of Chinese water torture for me. Drop, drop, drop, drop, pause . . . then, drop, drop, drop, pause . . . drop, drop. Will it ever stop? Probably not in my lifetime.

Shame shared by all priests

There is a deep sense of shame. Why do I feel shame? I feel shame because I identify with the Roman Catholic priesthood. I have never wanted to deny who or what I am. I never wanted to hide the fact of my being—being a priest. I was not ashamed of it.

As priests, we did what we could to build the brotherhood of priests. By our ordination we were granted respect and deference, not earned and not merited, but from the overflow of respect that other priests had won for us. We tried to honor their example and the fraternity. While we understood the flaws and failures, the sins and weaknesses of our brother priests, we stood with them and for them as they gave their best for the service of God and the church.

Now we find among us a growing number of priests who have be-

From John J. Dreese, "The Other Victims of Priest Pedophilia," *Commonweal*, April 22, 1994. Reprinted by permission of *Commonweal*.

trayed the confidence and trust that other priests have won for them. They have misused their positions of respect to defile, abuse, and steal the innocence of children and young people. We know that this is a sinful thing to do; the headlines and newscasts tell us that it is also a criminal thing to do. No wonder there is shame when we hear and read the news.

Roman Catholic priests have done this. If I identify with the Roman Catholic priesthood, I must be ashamed, saddened, and sickened by it all. To feel no shame, in light of all of this scandal, would be to feel a total lack of identification with the priesthood. In my guts I have always identified myself as a Catholic priest. Priesthood was not something I did, not a job, not a nine-to-five profession. Priesthood was my life; it was me. Priesthood is who I am. I cannot stop being me. For centuries the church has understood and taught that the person ordained undergoes an ontological change.

When the penance or treatment was completed, the pedophile was assigned to another parish, usually at a calculated distance from his last assignment.

If priesthood was only a job, a profession, a thing I did; if when the collar was off, office hours over, I was just the same as anyone else; if my private time was my own; if I was not the church's servant in the ministry of leadership, then perhaps I would not identify with the guilt and shame of this pedophile-priest scandal. But I cannot disassociate myself, since I do not believe in shedding the identity of being a priest.

The other way of avoiding the pain and the shame is to adopt the individualism pervasive in our culture. I could say, "What I do is my business and what they do is their business; it has nothing to do with me." That attitude is completely contrary to what biblical revelation teaches. I cannot accept, therefore, that mind-set. With the theology of priesthood I have internalized, there is no way to avoid the sense of shame and the feelings of hurt and embarrassment brought on me by my brother (would that I did not have to use the word) priests.

Mixed with the feelings of shame and embarrassment there is great anger. I am angry at the priest-pederasts and abusers. Why did they do what they did? They knew the meaning of celibacy, of chastity, continence. They knew the importance of innocence in the young and the scars of scandal to the community. Ignorance is not an alibi if they attended any kind of theological school. And they all did!

If they knew what they were doing but could not control a compulsion to act out, then they were clearly sick. At this point they had two choices: to get professional help or to get out of the priesthood. Professional help would have avoided further pain for all who eventually became involved. Getting out of the priesthood would have taken them away from the occasion of sin—principally, accessibility to youngsters among altar servers and school children. Leaving the priesthood would have taken away the possibility of scandal to the church. But it appears that the priest-offenders were not thinking about anyone but themselves. If pederasty, which I believe is the principal problem, is a self-centered and egotistical act and not brought under control, then it is all the more reason for shame and anger . . . and for pity.

Since the time of Augustine our tradition has taught us to hate the sin and love the sinner. That axiom is easy to say but hard to act on. It is especially difficult when it seems that the sinner in this case would bring down the entire world to satisfy his lusts or his sickness. He destroys the innocence of his victim, defiles the image of the church, betrays the trust of his fellow priests, all for his own sake.

This is a person I must love? Pity and disgust, I'm afraid, are the emotions I feel.

My anger is also directed at bishops. Why didn't they do something? It appears that they lectured priests about sin and suspended the guilty from sacramental ministry. Sometimes they sent them for medical treatment. But when the penance or treatment was completed, the pedophile was assigned to another parish, usually at a calculated distance from his last assignment.

After reassignment the pattern of sexual abuse often reoccurred. More innocent youths were victimized by the priest and the same pattern of penance and therapy and reassignment seems to have followed. Why was Father Pedophile not fired from the priesthood for good? The answer to that question is not clear to me. Looking back to the '60s and '70s the answer seems to have been, "A bishop cannot fire a priest." This was a common interpretation of canon law.

I remember consulting a canonist friend at The Catholic University of America about a problem priest from another diocese in the early '70s. He told me that one of the great problems in the church was the fact that there was no way that a bishop could fire a priest. Since Father Pedophile could not be fired, he was recycled. As a result, the pattern of abuse of children continued, and continued, and continued. For this, we now pay in many ways—ruined lives, shame, scandal, divisions in our parishes, and huge monetary fines imposed by the courts.

Reasons for inaction by other priests

What about me and my brother priests? Where were we when all this abuse was taking place? If to some extent we "knew" that priests were engaging in sexual abuse of children, why did we stand by and do nothing? What did we "know"? Thinking about these questions causes me to be angry at myself and at my brother priests.

There were certain priests that always had a cluster of boys around them. We knew that and comments about this situation were exchanged among priests. Usually, of course, there was never clear proof that Father was engaged in actual sexual abuse. Rash judgments were discouraged. We held to the admonition, prevalent in our society, that we were to give suspicious persons the benefit of the doubt. We wanted to expect only the best of our fellow priests.

In one of my early assignments the senior associate was known to be a friend of the boys in the parish. He always had a couple of junior high school boys with him. One evening, when I entered the rectory, this priest was in the living room with two of them. He told me that they were busy and asked me to leave the living room. I left, but I thought it strange that he would order me out to make room for two teen-agers. This same priest was considered a guru to teen-age boys in other parishes. Years later he was convicted of sexually abusing boys and served a prison sentence. What I suspected, but did not want to believe, had happened. Suspicion, however, is not proof. In today's climate I would confront the man. In 1963 I gave him the benefit of the doubt, and, as far as I know, so did everyone else.

I knew of another case where a priest classmate of mine was known to be an active homosexual who (it was said) acted out his sexual desires with young men. He was moved from assignment to assignment (it was rumored) because of his sexual activity. We were appalled to see him moved, allowing his sexual offenses to continue (that is, if the rumors were true). This occurred in the early '60s. As his peers we wished that he would leave the priesthood. Finally he left, to our relief, five or six years after ordination.

During this same period of time, a priest of my age openly admitted that he was active homosexually with an adult and that he had been active with high school boys. After his period of involvement with high school boys was discovered, he had been reassigned to another parish. He eventually chose to leave the priesthood, again to our relief. That the diocese was powerless in the face of such open perversion by some of its priests is almost impossible to comprehend today; yet, it was. Or, at least, it appeared that it was.

Other suspicions and surmises that have come to me in my thirty-four years as a priest did not seem worthy of aggressive action. I did not want to be judgmental. I knew homosexual priests who were living exemplary celibate lives. To accuse a person of pedophilia is a most serious charge. In retrospect, it might have been better to have acted aggressively in a couple of cases. I am angry at myself for this failure of judgment. Yet, even today certain priests in the diocese are under suspicion according to the clerical grapevine. What should be done with this "information" or "gossip"?

Today, of course, the media and TV, especially CNN, seem more and more ideological. "Roman Catholic priest," or "Father," are consistently used in their reporting. Rarely is the generic term of minister or simply, priest, used. Shots of the inside of a Roman Catholic church, of angelic altar boys in cassocks and surplices, and first communicants dressed in pure white dramatically highlight the bold betrayal of this crime. The anger I feel about the reporting of the priest pedophile cases needs no amplification. Cameras seem to search for ways to heighten the hurt, to magnify the mess. Is this responsible reporting, is it sensationalism, or is it Catholic bashing?

Punitive monetary awards to victims are unreasonable

I know it is in some sense unfair, but I harbor anger at juries for their excessive awards to victims of pedophiles. Do we really think as a society that monetary reward will make victims and their families whole again? The victims acted courageously in reporting the priests; I thank them for their courage. I wish they had done it long ago, closer to the time of the events. I agree with them that the priest-offender should be punished. I want them punished, too. I also understand the victims' need to tell their stories, and how important it is that they are finally able to speak out. I believe that the church should help them in every way possible.

But what constitutes genuine help? I question the huge sums of money the church is being asked to pay to victims for the crimes. If some victims hate the church, I can understand their feelings of vindictiveness and their desire for retribution. But if the goal is to recover health and wholeness, is pandering to desires for revenge and ratifying resentment real healing? Financial settlements seem like a simplistic and illusory response to a complex and emotional issue.

That the diocese was powerless in the face of such open perversion by some of its priests is almost impossible to comprehend today; yet, it was.

The abused children lost their innocence, much of the joy of childhood, their ability to have a positive self-image, and perhaps the possibility of healthy, loving sexual relationships as adults. These are horrible losses. No price tag can be placed on them. But should a diocese be held financially responsible for the criminal acts of individual priests, especially in cases where no negligence is involved?

If only we could get all the cases on the table once and for all, and be done with it. Must we all be tortured for what a James Porter did to children in North Attleboro, Fall River, New Mexico, and Minnesota? He has acknowledged his guilt and is in prison. This he deserves. But at what stage does the telling and re-telling of the story cease to be therapy, healthy, and helpful? Ever?

Changing views of pedophile-priests

I think everyone knows that in 1994 things are not what they were in 1960. Yet the media and those who hang on their reporting continue to judge 1960 actions by 1994 standards. Let me explain. Today, alcoholism is widely recognized as a disease. Thirty years ago alcoholism was considered a moral failure, a character defect, but not a disease. "The Pledge" was still being administered to those who drank too much. The affliction was not covered by health insurance. If alcoholics were taken to the hospital they were often placed in the psychiatric ward. Such treatment for alcoholism is now considered obsolete, even barbaric. Yet, it was once common practice. Other examples of significant differences in mores and medicine between 1960 and in 1994 could easily be cited.

In 1960, and even as late as 1980, pedophiles were treated, first, as *sinners*, and the treatment for sinners was administered to them. When the notion of sin no longer seemed adequate, pedophiles were considered to be sick, and the recommended treatment for psychologically sick people was prescribed. Today, abusers are treated as criminals and the recommended punishment for criminals is enforced.

Were the church and the bishops wrong to see pedophiles as sinners? Was it *really* moral negligence, or was the church naively imposing an erroneous diagnosis passed on to it?

When the church came to see pedophilia as a sickness, the bishops turned to experts in psychology and psychiatry who then knew little about effective treatment. Often, I am told, the professional counselors approved and recommended the priests' reassignment in the diocese. Was the church wrong to follow the advice of medical experts?

In 1960, and even as late as 1980, pedophiles were treated, first, as sinners, *and the treatment for sinners was administered to them.*

Today, we see pedophilia as a crime and seek punishment. The victims of the crime and their lawyers demand justice, and this involves large fees for attorneys. What are we doing by treating pedophilia primarily as a crime? Are we contributing to the recovery of the victim or the criminal? The damage remains. We may have made it more difficult for the pedophile to harm other innocent people, for a time, but there is recidivism among sexual deviants. Where are we in all of the murky mess? What counts for progress in this matter? I, for one, really don't know.

The effect on the priesthood

My anger is mixed with sadness. My sadness comes from the strong strains of selfishness, self-interest, revenge, vindictiveness, and sensationalism that linger in the air after every new report. Priests who have not committed the crimes are deeply hurt. A heavy pall hangs over the life of the priesthood. Priests find their duties to be difficult and joyless. Some are ashamed to wear a Roman collar. Others would like to wear a sign announcing, "I am not one of them." Phone calls are constantly exchanged about the most recent charges. Newspaper clippings are mailed by priests to their confreres detailing the most recent settlements. As a group we are slightly obsessed with this sad scandal.

This is all happening at a time when the priesthood seems to be threatened by a lack of candidates for ordination. Most priests are relatively old and have long borne the burden of the day. They are ready to slow down and pass the baton to the next generation. But there is no next generation. Their own lifetimes of service, fairly faithful for the great majority, are now tarnished and besmirched by the constant drone of the TV reporting: "A Roman Catholic priest of the diocese of _____ was charged today with sexually abusing a young boy while serving as associate pastor of Saint _____ Parish." Drop, drop. . . .

9

Some Priest Child Molesters Can Be Returned to Ministry

Stephen J. Rossetti

Stephen J. Rossetti is executive vice president and chief operating officer of the Saint Luke Institute, a rehabilitative care facility for priest sex offenders in Suitland, Maryland. He is the author of A Tragic Grace: The Catholic Church and Child Sexual Abuse.

Society's condemnation of child sexual molesters is based on the myths that pedophiles are "monsters" and are untreatable. Psychological counseling and drug treatment programs, coupled with after-treatment supervision, have been successful in treating many child abusers, particularly priests. Since congregations seem willing to accept treated priest offenders back into the community under certain conditions, the church should look for ways to reintegrate such priests into society.

What should be done with priests who sexually abuse minors? The very thought of returning them to ministry, or even to society, is appalling to many. "How can you even think of returning such men to positions of trust," people practically scream, "where they might abuse more of our children?" If this emotional protest does not suffice, the ground shifts to the legal argument. Attorneys counsel their bishops, "Returning a prior sex offender to ministry opens the church to unnecessary and severe monetary liability." If the priest offends again, one shudders to think of the financial cost.

Such arguments should not be dismissed. Sex offenders have indeed violated the trust they were given. If society has become wary, it is not without cause. And one cannot deny the legal and financial danger of returning a known sex offender to ministry. What could possibly justify such a risk?

As long as the question is argued on emotional or legal grounds, there will never be a cogent argument put forth to return sex offenders to min-

From Stephen J. Rossetti, "The Mark of Cain: Reintegrating Pedophiles," *America*, September 9, 1995. Reprinted with permission.

istry. It cannot be an emotionally popular decision. Child molesters have always been the "lowest of the low" in society, even in prisons. No one wants them. Likewise, the legal profession will continue to counsel taking the fewest risks. Returning known child molesters to ministry always carries some risk.

Banished from society

Looking to the secular world will provide little support for the reintegration of convicted sex offenders to society. In fact, the response of American society is becoming increasingly cynical and punitive. Parallels between the biblical story of Cain and the modern plight of child molesters come immediately to mind. Cain killed his brother, Abel. Just as God banished Cain from the soil and condemned him to be a "restless wanderer" on the earth (Gen. 4:11–12), so an increasing number of people would banish child molesters from living among the general population.

A rapidly expanding number of states require public notification of child molesters released from prison. New York State, for example, now notifies public school administrators about sex offenders who live in their area. In California a 900 number is being set up so that, for a fee of $4, a person can inquire whether someone they know has been convicted of child sexual abuse. In Louisiana, child sexual abusers are required by law to send written notices to their neighbors about their presence.

It is not surprising that these laws have spawned a number of violent acts. After "Megan's Law" was passed in New Jersey, a man who lived in the same residence as a sex offender was mistakenly beaten up after the offender's address was made public. In the State of Washington, a rapist's future residence was burned down when the community became aware that he was about to move in. It is not just the prison population that despises and beats up sex offenders.

This was Cain's fear. He cried out to God, "Since you have now banished me from the soil, and I must avoid your presence and become a restless wanderer on the earth, anyone may kill me at sight" (Gen. 4:14).

An increasing number of people would banish child molesters from living among the general population.

In a new twist, several states have recently passed laws allowing state officials to continue confinement of sexual offenders beyond their prison terms. Mitchell Gaff is currently confined in Washington State after serving a 10-year prison sentence. Under its new "sexual predator" law, the prosecutors sought an indefinite confinement for Mr. Gaff after his prison term expired. The proceedings are akin to those used in civil courts to confine the insane. Similar statutes have been passed in Wisconsin, New Jersey and Kansas.

This extreme social reaction to child molesters is not restricted to the United States. Viewing the comparable mood in Scotland, John Bancroft, M.D., commented in *Human Sexuality and Its Problems* (1989), "It is difficult to avoid the conclusion that in many cases the social reaction against the paedophile and the severity of the sentences imposed on him by the courts are out of proportion to the gravity of his offence."

Clerical prisons?

Not surprisingly, the Catholic Church is under similar pressure to ostracize priests known to have sexually molested minors. Like secular society, Catholic dioceses are becoming increasingly reluctant to take priest-offenders back into their ranks.

What currently happens to such clerics? If they refuse to request laicization, and many do refuse, the church has nowhere to put them. In one diocese I know of, the church sought a change in zoning to establish a house for such unassignable priests. The response of the secular community was overwhelmingly negative. The diocese tried again in another location and met with the same response. Eventually, it gave up.

But simply releasing all priests who have molested children into society unsupervised and untreated is not a good idea either. James Porter, a former priest, is a case in point. After offending against scores of minors in Massachusetts, he was voluntarily laicized by the church and released. Later, he was convicted of sexually molesting an unsuspecting family baby sitter in Minnesota.

In response to a mounting need, clerical "warehouses" are springing up. These are long-term care facilities, sometimes isolated from population centers, where these men reside. Warehouses offer a minimum of services and charge a modest daily fee to the sponsoring religious organization. At best, such places can be Christian communities of societal outcasts; at worst, they become clerical prisons.

Social lepers

One cannot help recalling the work of Father Damien among the lepers of Molokai. People with Hansen's disease did not request asylum. An 1865 law passed in Hawaii made it mandatory for victims of this disease to present themselves to the Board of Health. Some families would not hand over their sick members and tried to shelter them. The police were sent to hunt them down. Many lepers fled to the hills and to the caves. The police used bloodhounds to search them out.

Fearing contagion, Hawaii's government sent the victims of Hansen's disease to a settlement on the island of Molokai. The fear, a mixture of clinical facts and centuries of misinformation, fueled an irrational response to the disease. False legends and popular myths made those afflicted with Hansen's disease a dreaded people.

It might be argued that child molesters are different from those with Hansen's disease in that they are guilty of a crime, while lepers suffer from a physical disease. It is true that child molesters have committed a crime against vulnerable young people and should be subjected to the criminal justice system—for the sake of society and for their own sakes. More than one priest-offender has told me that he was glad he served time in prison for his offenses. He said he needed to repay a debt to society.

But, like lepers, those who sexually molest children almost always suffer from some sort of illness that spawns their aberrant behavior.

Pedophilia is a disease. Just as serious as physical illnesses, mental diseases should be diagnosed and treated by the best available clinical procedures.

The volatility of society's response to the child molester and the vengeance with which he is faced are striking. Few other heinous crimes engender the same response. There are no similar movements afoot to identify and restrict serial killers, drug dealers, child-beaters, cop-killers and psychopaths. Child sex molesters are singled out for particular loathing and punishment that is now being institutionalized by state governments. Truly, they bear the mark of Cain.

Hysteria fueled by myth

Just as the banishment of lepers was fueled by medieval myths, the hysteria surrounding child sexual abusers is exacerbated by myths about those who suffer from sexual deviancies. Child molesters incarnate our deepest childhood fears: We imagine them to be old, evil and malicious men. In our mind's eye, we see them as powerful and dark figures that lurk in the shadows and prey on the unsuspecting. The media described the child-molester priest James Porter as a "monster." One expected him to appear as a voracious, menacing figure who would strike terror in people's hearts. What appeared on television was a weak, frightened and confused man.

Our myths about child molesters come more from the projections of what lies within our own inner psyches than from the truth about who these men are. In fact, they are often ineffectual men whose dysfunctional upbringing did not afford them the chance to learn and act like competent, empowered adults. Successful treatment programs often include modules on assertiveness training; they are empowered to forge strong relationships with other adults. Child molesters are not potent men.

Similarly, the men who sexually abuse children are usually not old; this, too, is a myth. And perpetrators of child sexual abuse are, most often, not strangers; they either live within the home or they are neighbors. The best current research shows that the "average" child molester is young, well-educated, middle-class, sometimes married, usually Caucasian and employed in a stable job at a good salary. Richard I. Lanyon reported in the *Journal of Consulting and Clinical Psychology* (1986), "the child molester is most commonly a respectable, otherwise law-abiding person." Child molesters look a lot like us.

It is practically impossible to feel empathy for a menacing figure of power and evil. It is possible, however, to feel compassion for a friend and neighbor who was raised in a troubled household and then developed a serious sexual problem. There are child molesters who are dangerous and perhaps evil men. But the vast majority are troubled people, trapped in a web of denial, inner conflict, anger and fear. They wait for an understanding heart and a helping hand.

Recidivism rates

Another part of the reluctance to consider rehabilitation for those convicted of child sexual abuse is the common misconception that child molesters are clinically untreatable and compulsively driven to practice their perversion. This myth is sometimes repeated by mental health professionals.

There is some basis in fact for this pessimism. W.L. Marshall's research team noted in 1991 that "recidivism data up to the late 1960's are certainly not encouraging." The earliest treatment modalities often employed individual, insight-oriented psychotherapy. Just as this regimen has proven largely ineffective in treating alcoholics in the midst of their addiction, it has not been effective with child molesters. The perpetrators' denial, lack of motivation and tendencies to minimize their actions make them unsuitable candidates for such therapies. In addition, many early studies relied upon a highly impaired and compulsive group of incarcerated subjects who were more likely to re-offend.

In the last 20 years, however, newer treatment modalities have become available that have substantially increased the likelihood of successful treatment. W.L. Marshall's authoritative survey of the clinical literature in the *Clinical Psychology Review* (1991) concluded that comprehensive cognitive/behavioral programs and anti-androgen medications (e.g., Depo-Provera) were "unequivocally positive" in treating child molesters. The one caution: "Not all programs are successful and not all sex offenders profit from treatment."

But simply releasing all priests who have molested children into society unsupervised and untreated is not a good idea either.

What does "unequivocally positive" mean? In the late 1980s Fred Berlin, M.D., conducted a study of 173 treatment-compliant pedophiles and 126 treatment-noncompliant pedophiles at the Johns Hopkins Sexual Disorders Clinic. Five to six years after treatment began, the recidivism rate was 11.1 percent for the treatment-noncompliant group and only 2.9 percent for the treatment-compliant group. Most of the noncompliant group had received a significant amount of therapy but had ultimately been discharged for failure to attend sessions. Similarly, a Canadian study of 33 pedophiles used a sexual addictions model in treatment and had only a 3 percent recidivist rate over a five-year period.

Our experience at Saint Luke Institute confirms these findings. We have found that low doses (e.g., 250 mg. weekly) of Depo-Provera significantly lowers the serum testosterone level in males, and thus reduces the intensity of sexual urges, while having minimum side-effects. This form of "chemical castration" is reversible. It is used as a temporary means of reducing sexual drives in order to allow patients a period of calm in which to explore their sexuality and to implement more functional strategies in its management.

In the 10 years in which Saint Luke Institute has treated over 300 priests who have sexually molested minors, we currently know of only 2 who have relapsed into child sexual abuse. While it is likely that there are others whom we do not know about, our experience to date suggests that it is improbable that a priest will relapse if he has done well in residential treatment, complied with our 5-year after-care program and engaged in ongoing supervision and outpatient treatment.

It should be noted that published data on recidivism rates are not uniformly positive. In a 1989 survey, Lita Furby and her colleagues found a wide range of recidivism rates across many clinical studies. While there are reasons to be optimistic about the results of newer treatments, some caution and a healthy skepticism are not unwarranted.

Priest-perpetrators are often treatable

In her book *Sex Offenders: Approaches to Understanding and Management* (1988), Adele Mayer listed a number of factors that reduce the chances of successful treatment of sex-offenders: evidence of violent behavior, low I.Q., low capacity for insight, sexual abuse of very young children, organic brain deficits and severe character disorder. Our clinical experience supports Mayer's findings. Perpetrators who offend against younger prepubescent minors or who suffer from serious personality disorders, serious neuropsychological deficits, a rigid denial and/or a long history of compulsive abuse of many children are poor treatment risks. We would not likely recommend them to return to any form of ministry.

Fortunately, most of the priests who offend against minors do not have these negative treatment indicators. For example, Gene Abel's landmark study in 1987 found that 377 non-incarcerated child molesters who victimized children outside the home had an average of 72.72 victims and an average of 128.11 total acts of abuse. In contrast, in a Saint Luke Institute sample of 84 priest–child molesters, the average number of victims was 8.52 and the average number of total sexual contacts with minors was 32.14. Our data suggest that priest-perpetrators of child sexual abuse are likely to commit fewer acts against fewer victims.

The "average" child molester is young, well-educated, middle-class, sometimes married, usually Caucasian and employed in a stable job at a good salary.

In fact, priest-offenders have tended to be intelligent, high-functioning men, many of whom had otherwise exemplary ministries. For example, in a sample of 224 priest–child molesters at Saint Luke Institute, the average I.Q. score was 122. This places them in the upper 7 percent of the general population. It would be statistically misleading to compare the likelihood of treatment success on these higher-functioning priests using modern treatment modalities with outdated methods used on incarcerated, lower-functioning patients.

Similarly, Fred Berlin, M.D., notes that "media can distort public perceptions of treatment outcome" for sex offenders and such distortions have aided in "creating a climate of opinion that is unjustifiably biased against psychiatric care."

Will people take them back?

But even if further clinical studies show that many priest-perpetrators are at minimal risk for re-offending, social stereotypes and myths will remain. Will church members be willing to take some of them back into ministry?

With the help of Twenty-Third Publications, I surveyed 1,810 active Roman Catholics from the United States and Canada (87 percent of whom were in active lay ministries within their churches, the rest priests, sisters or religious brothers). They were presented with the statement: "A priest who abuses children should *not* be allowed to return to ministry." The responses were as follows:

A priest who abuses children should *not* be allowed to return to ministry.

42% agree   31% unsure   27% disagree

The survey results indicated that active Catholics are divided on the issue. A solid number of people are opposed to returning priest-offenders to ministry. Of the 42 percent who opposed their return, more than half indicated they felt strongly that child molesters should not be returned. Any bishop or superior who returns a priest-offender to ministry will have to bear in mind, therefore, that a significant number of people will not agree with his decision.

Our data suggest that priest-perpetrators of child sexual abuse are likely to commit fewer acts against fewer victims.

The above question left many additional questions unanswered, such as: "What sort of ministry would he be returning to?" and "Under what conditions?" In the same survey, therefore, I asked people to respond to a second statement: "I would accept a former priest–child abuser into *my parish* if he had undergone psychological treatment and was being supervised by another priest." This places additional conditions on his return and brings the question home to the respondent: The priest-perpetrator will be coming into *your* parish. Participants responded as follows:

I would accept a former priest–child abuser into *my parish* if he had undergone psychological treatment and was being supervised by another priest.

51% agree   27% unsure   22% disagree

The change in the survey responses from the first to the second statement is important. When a priest-offender has gone through treatment and is being supervised, a majority of active Catholics would accept the priest back into their own parishes. The percentage who would *not* want him back dropped from 42 percent to 22 percent. It is likely that if even more conditions were placed upon the returning priest, such as limiting him to ministries that did not involve minors, an increasing percentage would be supportive of his return.

Educational efforts and disseminating new data on recidivism and successes in treatment will be important, not only for Catholic leaders, but for the general community. In addition, the data suggest that there will be increasing support from Catholics for a return to ministry for some offenders if the conditions of the decision are clear and strict requirements are imposed upon the priest's life and ministry.

Other considerations

Perhaps the most unhealthy myth regarding child molesters is that they are all the same. In fact, adults who sexually molest children are clinically and behaviorally quite different. I recall a 26-year-old priest who, in an impulsive act, fondled a 16-year-old girl. Clinically, he was a very different man from a 50-year-old narcissistic priest who coerced and seduced scores of 12-year-old boys. I suggest that it would be inappropriate, even hazardous, for society and the church to deal with them in exactly the same manner.

After several years of working with dioceses and religious orders considering a return to ministry for former sex offenders, the following factors have emerged:

• *Clinical diagnosis and abuse history.* As noted above, Adele Mayer outlined several factors contributing to poor-risk candidates. Priests with few of these negative indicators would probably be a better risk. For example, a priest who abused older children, had few victims, did not use overt violence and was without a severe character disorder or organic brain deficits would be a better candidate for a return to ministry. On the other hand, a priest who abused scores of pre-pubescent children, sometimes employed violence and had a serious personality disorder would be a poor risk for any future ministry.

I would not recommend that a priest-perpetrator ever return to a ministry that directly involves minors.

• *Quality of treatment and response to treatment.* Before considering a return to ministry, it will be important for the perpetrator to have gone through and done reasonably well in a program that specializes in treating sex offenders. Sometimes perpetrators are placed in therapy with well-intentioned counselors who are not trained in dealing with child molesters. These therapists can be manipulated by the offenders and may end up colluding in their patients' denial and projection of guilt. A skilled sex offenders' program will assist the patient in honestly acknowledging his problem, taking personal responsibility for the harm he has caused and committing himself to a program of recovery. Without achieving these and other therapeutic goals, the perpetrator is not ready to re-engage in ministry. A good treatment outcome will be important for a return to ministry.

• *After-care program.* It is vital that the perpetrator's recovery be an ongoing process that extends well beyond the initial treatment. Such after-care programs are usually multi-year, structured and comprehensive, including ongoing individual and group therapy, regular meetings with a support group and periodic assessments of progress. Like any mental illness, a successful recovery for sex offenders is a process that requires dedication and hard work. This comprehensive program should be in place and functioning before he returns to ministry.

• *Availability of supervision and ministry not involving minors.* Even with a positive treatment outcome and a comprehensive after-care program, I would not recommend that a priest-perpetrator *ever* return to a ministry that directly involves minors. I believe it would be a pastorally imprudent decision to place the perpetrator back into a significant position of trust with minors. It will be important to find a ministry that includes a different age-group and that his ministry be supervised in the external forum by someone who is aware of his background. Regular sessions with this supervisor will include frank discussions of any incidental contact with minors and related behaviors.

To reintegrate child molesters into our society will require us to face and overcome our own fears.

• *Other pastoral considerations.* There may be extenuating circumstances that affect the possibility of the priest's return to ministry. For example, has there been considerable public notoriety about his case? Are victims or victims' families threatening legal action if he returns to ministry? Are there a number of past victims that have not yet come forward who would be affected by seeing him in a ministerial role? These and other similar pastoral considerations must be taken into account by any bishop or superior who is evaluating the ministerial prospects of a priest-offender.

• *Consider a waiting period.* Sometimes a priest has done well in treatment but the treating facility and/or the diocese believe the priest is not yet ready to return to ministry. If questions persist about the stability of his recovery, a period of one to three years of time away from ministry might strengthen the priest's recovery and provide assurances of his perseverance. At the end of this time, his superiors might then reassess his suitability for some sort of ministry.

Overall, I believe it would be a pastorally prudent decision for a bishop to return to a limited ministry a priest-perpetrator who does well in treatment, has few negative treatment indicators, has a comprehensive after-care program in place, is supervised in the external forum and is placed in a ministry that does not involve minors. There are more than a few men who have returned and are quietly serving under these circumscribed conditions.

Cain's protection

The mark of Cain was not meant as a sign of Cain's sin or of his banishment from the soil. It was given by God himself as a sign of divine protection. Because of the effects of his sin, Cain's burden was too heavy for him to bear. God showed compassion and protected Cain, despite the heinousness of his crime.

The child molester has committed a heinous crime against our children and against society. If the offender is a priest, his crime is all the greater. Like Cain, he is to be subjected to punishment. But he should also bear the sign of our protection as a man who has been wounded himself and is in need of our assistance.

Newer psychological and pharmacological treatments have assisted many offenders to discover healthy and chaste living. More than one priest-perpetrator has privately confided, "Treatment saved my life." Ministerial decisions regarding priest-offenders should take into account a variety of clinical and pastoral factors. After treatment, some of these men are good candidates for a limited, supervised ministry not involving children. Others will need an extended period of non-ministerial time to demonstrate the ability to live chastely. Unfortunately, there will always be a few who remain untreatable and will be an unacceptable risk for any sort of ministry. For them, supervised living without public ministry is all that is currently available.

A Christian perspective suggests the need for society and church to take a reasoned response with an informed compassion and a willingness to delve into the complexities. But society hates and fears men who sexually abuse minors. We stereotype them; we claim they are all incorrigible; we wish to mark them as people not like ourselves. These men tap a deep well of fear and anger that goes beyond the facts of their crime. To reintegrate child molesters into our society will require us to face and overcome our own fears. To live in peace with child molesters will mean to let go of some of our own inner angers.

Perhaps their presence in society can ultimately be healing for us. They challenge us to face an unconscious and primal darkness within humankind. Our inability to face this darkness causes us to stereotype and banish all who embody our estranged dis-passions. In the past, this process spawned Molokai and a host of other human prisons. Today, we are banishing the child molester.

Organizations to Contact

The editors have compiled the following list of organizations concerned with the issues debated in this book. The descriptions are derived from materials provided by the organizations. All have publications or information available for interested readers. The list was compiled on the date of publication of the present volume; names, addresses, phone and fax numbers, and e-mail and Internet addresses may change. Be aware that many organizations take several weeks or longer to respond to inquiries, so allow as much time as possible.

American Academy of Child and Adolescent Psychiatry (AACAP)
3615 Wisconsin Ave. NW
Washington, DC 20016
(202) 966-7300
fax: (202) 966-2891
Internet: http://www.aacap.org

The AACAP is an association of psychiatrists who specialize in child and adolescent psychiatry. In addition to professional publications, it publishes the Facts for Families series, a collection of information sheets on psychiatric disorders affecting children and adolescents. Titles include "Child Sexual Abuse" and "Child Abuse—the Hidden Bruises."

American Bar Association (ABA)
Center for Children and the Law
750 N. Lake Shore Dr.
Chicago, IL 60611
(312) 988-5000
e-mail: ctrchildlaw@abanet.org
Internet: http://www.abanet.org

The ABA Center for Children and the Law aims to improve the quality of life for children through advances in law and public policy. It publishes the monthly *ABA Juvenile and Child Welfare Law Reporter* and specializes in providing information on legal matters related to the protection of children.

American Professional Society on the Abuse of Children (APSAC)
407 S. Dearborn St., Suite 1300
Chicago, IL 60605
(312) 554-0166
Internet: http://www.apsac.org

The APSAC is dedicated to improving the coordination of services in the fields of child abuse prevention, treatment, and research. It publishes a quarterly newsletter, the *Advisor*, and the *Journal of Interpersonal Violence*.

Child Abuse and Disabled Project (CADP)
The Lexington Center
30th Ave. at 75th St.
Jackson Heights, NY 11370
(718) 899-8800

The CADP works to protect children who are especially vulnerable to abuse because of disabilities and addresses the challenges encountered in interventions with such children. The project offers reprints of articles on these subjects and lists of professionals and organizations active in these areas.

Child Assault Prevention Project (CAP)
National Assault Prevention Center (NAPC)
PO Box 02005
Columbus, OH 43202
(614) 291-2540

The National Assault Prevention Center was founded to prevent violence through curriculum development, research, and education. Its Child Assault Prevention Project provides abuse prevention services to children of all ages, children with special needs, parents, teachers, and professionals. The NAPC and CAP publish brochures, videos, booklets, and books such as *New Strategies for Free Children*, a manual for running a CAP project.

Child Protection Program Foundation
7441 Marvin D. Love Freeway, Suite 200
Dallas, TX 75237
(214) 709-0300

The foundation was created to help prevent the criminal neglect and physical, emotional, and sexual abuse of children in America. Its advocacy efforts include distribution of educational materials, including the *Child Protection Guide* and *Victim Resources Manual*.

Child Welfare League of America (CWLA)
440 First St. NW, Suite 310
Washington, DC 20001-2085
(202) 638-2952
fax: (202) 638-4004
e-mail: books@swla.org
Internet: http://www.cwla.org

The Child Welfare League of America is an association of more than seven hundred public and private agencies and organizations devoted to improving the lives of children. CWLA publications include the book *Tender Mercies: Inside the World of a Child Abuse Investigator*, the quarterly magazine *Children's Voice*, and the bimonthly journal *Child Welfare*.

False Memory Syndrome Foundation
3401 Market St., Suite 130
Philadelphia, PA 19104
(800) 568-8882
(215) 387-1865
fax: (215) 387-1917
Internet: http://advicom.net/~fitz/fmsf/

The foundation believes that many "delayed memories" of sexual abuse are the result of false memory syndrome (FMS). In FMS, patients in therapy "recall" childhood abuse that never occurred. The foundation seeks to discover reasons for the spread of FMS, works for the prevention of new cases, and aids FMS victims, including those falsely accused of abuse. The foundation publishes a newsletter and various papers and distributes articles and information on FMS.

Family Research Laboratory (FRL)
University of New Hampshire
Durham, NH 03824-3586
(603) 862-1888
fax: (603) 862-1122
e-mail: shf@christa.unh.edu
Internet: http://www.edu/frlo/regbroch.htm

The FRL is an independent research group that studies the causes and consequences of family violence, including physical and sexual abuse of children, and the connections between family violence and other social problems. A bibliography of works on these subjects, produced by staff members under the sponsorship of the University of New Hampshire, is available from the FRL.

Family Violence and Sexual Assault Institute (FVSAI)
1310 Clinic Dr.
Tyler, TX 75701
(903) 595-6600
Internet: http://ericps.ed.vivc.edu/npin/reswork/workorgs/fvsainst.html

The FVSAI networks among people and agencies involved in studying, treating, protecting, or otherwise dealing with violent or abusive families. The FVSAI maintains a computerized database that includes unpublished or hard-to-find articles and papers, which are available for copying and postage charges. Publications include the bibliographies *Sexual Abuse/Incest Survivors* and *Child Physical Abuse/Neglect* and the quarterly *Family Violence and Sexual Assault Bulletin.*

Federation on Child Abuse and Neglect
134 S. Swan St.
Albany, NY 12210
(518) 445-1273

The federation works to prevent all types of child abuse through public education and advocacy. It offers brochures such as *What Kids Should Know About Child Abuse and Neglect*, booklets such as *Child Sexual Abuse Guidelines for Health Professionals*, fact sheets, and reprinted articles.

For Kids' Sake
31676 Railroad Canyon Rd.
Canyon Lake, CA 92380
(714) 244-9001

For Kids' Sake is dedicated to the prevention of child abuse through education and intervention. It believes that the problems of parenting are best solved by the community. For Kids' Sake maintains a large research library on this subject and offers brochures on parenting and child safety; molestation-prevention programs and curricula; and educational materials for medical, law enforcement, and teaching personnel.

Incest Resources, Inc. (IR)
Cambridge Women's Center
46 Pleasant St.
Cambridge, MA 02139
(617) 354-8807

IR provides educational and resource materials for incest survivors. The IR legal packet is a series of articles and resource listings related to civil prosecution of incest offenders. A self-addressed stamped envelope (two first-class stamps) must accompany requests for information.

Incest Survivors Resource Network International (ISRNI)
PO Box 7375
Las Cruces, NM 88006-7375
(505) 521-4260
fax: (505) 521-3723
e-mail: ISRNI@zianet.com
Internet: http://www.zianet.com/ISRNI/

The ISRNI stresses awareness of male incest victims of female abusers and of the concept of emotional incest. It offers bibliographies and networking information that enables survivors of child sexual abuse to contact similar organizations throughout the United States.

Kempe National Center for the Prevention and Treatment of Child Abuse and Neglect
1205 Oneida St.
Denver, CO 80220-2944
(303) 321-3963
Internet: http://www.social.com/health/nhic/data/hr1100/hr1106.html

The Kempe National Center is a resource for research on all forms of child abuse and neglect. It is committed to multidisciplinary approaches to improve recognition, treatment, and prevention of abuse. The center's resource library offers a catalog of books, booklets, information packets, and articles on child sexual abuse issues.

National Center for Missing and Exploited Children (NCMEC)
2101 Wilson Blvd., Suite 550
Arlington, VA 22201-3052
(800) THE LOST
(703) 739-0321
Internet: http://www.missingkids.org

The NCMEC serves as a clearinghouse of information on missing and exploited children and coordinates child protection efforts with the private sector. A number of publications on these issues are available, including guidelines for parents whose children are testifying in court, help for abused children, and booklets such as *Children Traumatized in Sex Rings* and *Child Molesters: A Behavioral Analysis*.

National Center for Prosecution of Child Abuse
American Prosecutors Research Institute
99 Canal Center Plaza, Suite 510
Alexandria, VA 22314
(703) 739-0321

The center seeks to improve the investigation and prosecution of child abuse cases. A clearinghouse on child abuse laws and court reforms, the center supports research on reducing courtroom trauma for child victims. It publishes a monthly newsletter, *Update,* as well as monographs, bibliographies, special reports, and a manual for prosecutors, *Investigation and Prosecution of Child Abuse.*

National Committee for Prevention of Child Abuse (NCPCA)
332 S. Michigan Ave., Suite 1600
Chicago, IL 60604-4357
(312) 663-3520
fax: (312) 939-8962
Internet: http://www.childabuse.org

The NCPCA's mission is to prevent abuse in all its forms. The committee distributes and publishes materials on a variety of topics, including child abuse and child abuse prevention. A free catalog is available from NCPCA Publications Department, PO Box 94283, Chicago, IL 60690.

National Institute of Justice (NIJ)
U.S. Department of Justice, National Criminal Justice Reference Service
PO Box 6000
Rockville, MD 20849-6000
(800) 851-3420
(301) 251-5500
Internet: http://www.ncjrs.org/unjust/inijhome.htm

The NIJ is the research and development agency of the U.S. Department of Justice established to prevent and reduce crime and to improve the criminal justice system. Among its publications is the report *When the Victim Is a Child,* which reviews new research on the consequences of child sexual abuse and the capabilities of children as witnesses.

National Resource Center on Child Abuse and Neglect (NRCCAN)
63 Inverness Dr. East
Englewood, CO 80112-5117
(800) 227-5242

The NRCCAN identifies and organizes resources on child abuse and neglect, disseminates information, and coordinates with the National Resource Center on Child Sexual Abuse and the National Clearinghouse on Child Abuse and Neglect Information. It responds to requests for information and attempts to identify emerging issues and developmental needs in the field of child protection.

National Resource Center on Child Sexual Abuse
106 Lincoln St.
Huntsville, AL 35801
(800) 543-7006

The center is funded by the U.S. Department of Health and Human Services' National Center on Child Abuse and Neglect and is operated by the National Children's Advocacy Center. In addition to its toll-free information line, the center publishes a newsletter, information papers, monographs, and bibliographies.

National Victims Resource Center (NVRC)
PO Box 6000
Rockville, MD 20850
(800) 627-6872

The NVRC is a primary source of information on crime victims as well as research and statistics on child abuse. It distributes a child abuse information package and several pamphlets, such as *Child Sexual Abuse Victims and Their Treatment* and *Police and Child Abuse.*

NOW Legal Defense and Education Fund
99 Hudson St., 12th Fl.
New York, NY 10013
(212) 925-6635
fax: (212) 226-1066
Internet: http://www.nowldef.org

The NOW Legal Defense and Education Fund is a branch of the National Organization for Women, an organization that seeks to end discrimination against women. The fund offers a publications list and a legal resources kit on incest and child sexual abuse.

The Safer Society Foundation
PO Box 340-1
Brandon, VT 05733-0340
(802) 247-3132
Internet: http://www.safersociety.org

The Safer Society Foundation, a project of the New York State Council of Churches, is a national research, advocacy, and referral center for the prevention of sexual abuse of children and adults. The Safer Society Press publishes studies and books on treatment for sexual abuse victims and offenders and on the prevention of sexual abuse.

Sex Information and Education Council of the United States (SIECUS)
130 W. 42nd St., Suite 350
New York, NY 10036-7802
(212) 819-9770
fax: (212) 819-9776
e-mail: siecus@siecus.org
Internet: http://www.siecus.org

SIECUS is a clearinghouse for information on sexuality, with a special interest in sex education. It publishes sex education curricula, the bimonthly newsletter *SIECUS Report*, and fact sheets on sex education issues. Its articles, bibliographies, and book reviews often address the role of education in identifying, reducing, and preventing sexual abuse.

United Fathers of America (UFA)
Smith Tower, Suite 1521
506 Second Ave.
Seattle, WA 98104-2311
(800) 689-7949
fax: (206) 623-3933
e-mail: info@ufa.com
Internet: http://www.ufa.com

UFA is primarily a support group for men whose former spouses have falsely accused them of sexually abusing their children. Although the organization believes in protecting children from abuse, it does not believe that fathers should be forced to endure the emotional and psychological trauma caused by false accusations. UFA answers specific questions and suggests articles and studies that illustrate its position.

VOCAL/National Association of State VOCAL Organizations (NASVO)
PO Box 1314
Orangevale, CA 95662
(800) 745-8778
(916) 863-7470

Victims of Child Abuse Laws (VOCAL) provides information and data, conducts research, and offers emotional support for those who have been falsely accused of child abuse. The NASVO maintains a library of research on child abuse and neglect issues, focusing on legal, mental health, social, and medical issues, and will provide photocopies of articles for a fee. It publishes the bimonthly newsletter *NASVO News*.

VOICES in Action, Inc.
PO Box 148309
Chicago, IL 60614
(312) 327-1500

Victims of Incest Can Emerge Survivors (VOICES) provides assistance to victims of incest and child sexual abuse and promotes awareness about the prevalence of incest. It publishes a bibliography and the newsletter the *Chorus*, and it offers reprints of papers and articles such as "Myths of Male Sexual Abuse: Factors in Underreporting."

Women Against Rape (WAR)/Child Watch
PO Box 346
Collingswood, NJ 08108
(609) 858-7800

The WAR/Child Watch offices handle information requests for Society's League Against Molestation (SLAM), an organization that researches social, psychological, and legal aspects of molestation, monitors court cases, and suggests legislation to prevent abuse. WAR/Child Watch's publications include brochures such as *Incest/Molestation* and statistics on sexual assault.

Bibliography

Books

Judith L. Alpert — *Sexual Abuse Recalled: Treating Trauma in the Era of the Recovered Memory Debate*. Northvale, NJ: Jason Aronson, 1995.

Louise Armstrong — *Rocking the Cradle of Sexual Politics: What Happened When Women Said Incest*. Reading, MA: Addison-Wesley, 1994.

Matthew Colton and Maurice Vanstone — *Betrayal of Trust: Sexual Abuse by Men Who Work with Children—in Their Own Words*. New York: Free Association Books, 1996.

Lela B. Costin, Howard Jacob Karger, and David Stoesz — *The Politics of Child Abuse in America*. New York: Oxford University Press, 1995.

Linda Katherine Cutting — *Memory Slips: A Memoir of Music and Healing*. New York: HarperCollins, 1997.

Jennifer J. Freyd — *Betrayal Trauma: The Logic of Forgetting Childhood Abuse*. Cambridge, MA: Harvard University Press, 1996.

Richard J. Gelles — *The Book of David: How Preserving Families Can Cost Children's Lives*. New York: BasicBooks, 1996.

Eliana Gil — *Treating Abused Adolescents*. New York: Guildford, 1996.

Pat Gilmartin — *Rape, Incest, and Child Sexual Abuse: Consequences and Recovery*. New York: Garland, 1994.

Lawrence A. Greenfield — *Child Victimizers: Violent Offenders and Their Victims*. U.S. Department of Justice, Office of Justice Programs, Bureau of Justice Statistics. Washington, DC: GPO, 1996.

Mic Hunter, ed. — *Adult Survivors of Sexual Abuse: Treatment Innovations*. Thousand Oaks, CA: Sage Publications, 1995.

Philip Jenkins — *Pedophiles and Priests: Anatomy of a Contemporary Crisis*. New York: Oxford University Press, 1996.

Elizabeth Loftus and Katherine Ketcham — *The Myth of Repressed Memory: False Memories and Allegations of Sexual Abuse*. New York: St. Martin's Press, 1995.

Jennifer L. Manlowe — *Faith Born of Seduction: Sexual Trauma, Body Image, and Religion*. New York: New York University Press, 1995.

Matthew Parynik Mendel — *The Male Survivor: The Impact of Sexual Abuse*. Thousand Oaks, CA: Sage Publications, 1995.

Debbie Nathan and Michael Snedeker — *Satan's Silence: Ritual Abuse and the Making of a Modern American Witch Hunt*. New York: BasicBooks, 1996.

91

James Randell Noblitt and Pamela Sue Perskin	*Cult and Ritual Abuse: Its History, Anthropology, and Recent Discovery in Contemporary America.* Westport, CT: Praeger, 1995.
Richard Ofshe and Ethan Watters	*Making Monsters: False Memories, Psychotherapy, and Sexual Hysteria.* New York: Scribner's, 1994.
Mark Pendergrast	*Victims of Memory: Incest Accusations and Shattered Lives.* Hinesburg, VT: Upper Access, 1995.
Douglas W. Pryor	*Unspeakable Acts: Why Men Sexually Abuse Children.* New York: New York University Press, 1996.
Ginger Rhodes and Richard Rhodes	*Trying to Get Some Dignity: Stories of Triumph over Childhood Abuse.* New York: William Morrow, 1996.
Stephen J. Rosetti	*A Tragic Grace: The Catholic Church and Child Sexual Abuse.* Collegeville, MN: Liturgical Press, 1996.
Michael Ryan	*Secret Life: An Autobiography.* New York: Pantheon Books, 1995.
Lenore Terr	*Unchained Memories: True Stories of Traumatic Memories, Lost and Found.* New York: BasicBooks, 1994.
U.S. Dept. of Justice	*Sexually Transmitted Diseases and Child Sexual Abuse: Portable Guides to Investigating Child Abuse.* Office of Justice Programs, Office of Juvenile Justice and Delinquency Prevention. Washington, DC: GPO, 1996.
Juliann Whetsell-Mitchell	*Rape of the Innocent: Understanding and Preventing Child Sexual Abuse.* Washington, DC: Accelerated Development, 1995.
Debra Whitcomb et al.	*The Emotional Effects of Testifying on Sexually Abused Children.* U.S. Department of Justice, Office of Justice Programs, National Institute of Justice. Washington, DC: GPO, 1994.
Michael D. Yapko	*Suggestions of Abuse: True and False Memories of Childhood Sexual Trauma.* New York: Simon & Schuster, 1994.

Periodicals

Jerry Adler and Peter Annin	"Too Dangerous to Set Free?" *Newsweek*, December 9, 1996.
Trevor Armbrister	"Justice Gone Crazy," *Reader's Digest*, January 1994.
Trevor Armbrister	"Witch Hunt in Wenatchee," *Reader's Digest*, July 1996.
Tom Bethell	"Sex, Lies, and Kinsey: Exposing the Father of Child Abuse," *American Spectator*, May 1996.
Mikkel Borch-Jacobsen	"Sybil—the Making of a Disease: An Interview with Dr. Herbert Spiegel," *New York Review of Books*, April 24, 1997.
Jim Breig	"Labeling Sex Offenders Won't Protect the Children," *U.S. Catholic*, November 1996.
Barry Came	"Are Your Kids Safe?" *Maclean's*, February 10, 1997.

Margaret Carlson   "The Sex-Crime Capital," *Time*, November 13, 1995.

Canice Connors   "The Moment After Suffering," *Commonweal*, October 21, 1994.

Peter Davis   "The Sex Offender Next Door," *New York Times Magazine*, July 28, 1996.

Midge Decter   "Megan's Law and the 'New York Times,'" *Commentary*, October 1994.

Mary Eberstadt   "Pedophilia Chic," *Weekly Standard*, June 17, 1996. Available from 1211 Avenue of the Americas, New York, NY 10036.

Maija Elina   "In the Family of God," *Humanist*, July/August 1996.

Nancy Hass   "Margaret Kelly Michaels Wants Her Innocence Back," *New York Times Magazine*, September 10, 1995.

Jim Kershner   "A Witch Hunt in Wenatchee?" *American Journalism Review*, June 1996.

Joe Klein   "The Predator Problem," *Newsweek*, April 29, 1996.

Larry Don McQuay   "The Case for Castration, Part 1," *Washington Monthly*, May 1992.

Gary Pool   "Sex, Science, and Kinsey: A Conversation with Dr. John Bancroft," *Humanist*, September/October 1996.

Dorothy Rabinowitz   "Wenatchee: A True Story," *Wall Street Journal*, September 29, 1995.

Dorothy Rabinowitz   "Wenatchee: A True Story—II," *Wall Street Journal*, October 13, 1995.

Joannie M. Schrof   "Moving Beyond True and False," *U.S. News & World Report*, January 27, 1997.

Ruth Shalit   "Witch Hunt," *New Republic*, June 19, 1995.

Carol Smolenski   "Sex Tourism and the Sexual Exploitation of Children," *Christian Century*, November 15, 1995.

Cathy Spatz Widom   "Childhood Sexual Abuse and Its Criminal Consequences," *Society*, May/June 1996.

World Press Review   "New Focus on an Ancient Evil: Fighting the Child Sex Trade," November 1996.

Index

a.1

BOOK WORMS

Ready for School
We Listen

Listos para ir a la escuela
Escuchamos

Sharon Gordon

Marshall Cavendish
Benchmark
New York

We listen.

❖

Escuchamos.

We go to school.

We listen.

❖

Vamos a la escuela.

Escuchamos.

We see the teacher.

We listen.

———————◆———————

Vemos a la maestra.

Escuchamos.

We read a book.
We listen.

Leemos un libro.
Escuchamos.

We show and tell.

We listen.

❖

Mostramos y explicamos.

Escuchamos.

11

We play games.
We listen.

---❖---

Jugamos.
Escuchamos.

We talk to friends.

We listen.

———◆———

Hablamos con amigos.

Escuchamos.

15

We see a play.
We listen.

Vemos una obra de teatro.
Escuchamos.

We walk home.
We listen!

Caminamos a casa.
¡Escuchamos!

19

We Listen

games
jugar

play
obra de teatro

read
leer

school
escuela

20

show and tell
mostrar y explicar

talk
hablar

teacher
maestra

walk
caminar

Index

Índice

About the Author
Datos biográficos de la autora

Sharon Gordon has written many books for young children. She has always worked as an editor. Sharon and her husband Bruce have three children, Douglas, Katie, and Laura, and one spoiled pooch, Samantha. They live in Midland Park, New Jersey.

❖

Sharon Gordon ha escrito muchos libros para niños. Siempre ha trabajado como editora. Sharon y su esposo Bruce tienen tres niños, Douglas, Katie y Laura, y una perra consentida, Samantha. Viven en Midland Park, Nueva Jersey.

With thanks to Nanci Vargus, Ed.D. and Beth Walker Gambro, reading consultants

Marshall Cavendish Benchmark
99 White Plains Road
Tarrytown, New York 10591-9001
www.marshallcavendish.us

Library of Congress Cataloging-in-Publication Data

Gordon, Sharon.
We listen = Escuchamos / Sharon Gordon. — Bilingual ed.
p. cm. — (Bookworms, ready for school = Listos para ir a la escuela)
Includes index.
ISBN-13: 978-0-7614-2439-0 (bilingual edition)
ISBN-10: 0-7614-2439-3 (bilingual edition)
ISBN-13: 978-0-7614-2359-1 (Spanish edition)
ISBN-10: 0-7614-1991-8 (English edition)
1. Education—Juvenile literature. 2. School day—Juvenile literature. 3. Listening—Juvenile literature. I. Title. II. Title: Escuchamos.

LB1556.G6718 2006
372.18—dc22
2006018214

Spanish Translation and Text Composition by Victory Productions, Inc.
www.victoryprd.com

Photo Research by Anne Burns Images

Cover Photo by *Corbis*/Brownie Harris

The photographs in this book are used with permission and through the courtesy of:
Corbis: pp. 1, 7, 11, 21 (top l), 21 (bottom l) Ariel Skelley; p. 3 Jon Feingersh; pp. 5, 20 (bottom r) Michael Keller; pp. 9, 20 (bottom l) Rob Lewine; pp. 13, 20 (top l) Royalty Free; pp. 15, 21 (top r) Peter M. Fisher; pp. 17, 20 (top r) LWA-Dann Tardif; pp. 19, 21 (bottom r) Philip Gould.

Printed in Malaysia
1   3   5   6   4   2